The Charismatic Phenomenon

The Charismatic Phenomenon

Peter Masters
John C Whitcomb

THE WAKEMAN TRUST ✱ **LONDON**

© 1982 Peter Masters & John C Whitcomb
First published 1982 in magazine format,
reprinted 1982, 1983, 1984, 1986
This revised and expanded edition
first published June 1988
Second printing October 1989

ISBN 1 870855 01 9

Cover design by Andrew Sides

*Printed in Great Britain for the Wakeman Trust, Elephant
& Castle, London SE1 6SD by J W Arrowsmith, Bristol.*

Contents

Introduction

SINCE THE HOLY SPIRIT came down on the newly-formed Church of Jesus Christ on the Day of Pentecost, two thousand years of Christian witness have passed, and momentous battles have been fought between the devil and the Church. Satan has launched brutal physical persecutions from without, and by infiltration has campaigned to overthrow evangelical doctrine from within. But, by the mighty power of the Spirit, a true Church — made up of myriad living congregations throughout the world — has prevailed and grown.

The history of the Church is studded with countless triumphs of grace, seen in mighty awakenings and periods when the wonderful light of God has streamed from His unchanging and inerrant Word. Yet all these glorious events of the Spirit have occurred, including all the battles of persecution, reformation and revival, without the benefit of the charismatic movement.

Pentecostalism began only towards the end of the 19th century, and never became more than a tiny part of the Christian witness scene for the first fifty years of its existence. The modern charismatic movement did not even begin to emerge from Pentecostalism until around 1955. At the present time it has existed for less than 40 years of the nearly 2,000 years which have elapsed since Pentecost.

For all this, charismatic teachers and authors are undaunted in their claim to have rediscovered the lost doctrines of the Spirit. They contemptuously sweep aside the witness of the centuries as a witness conducted in semi-darkness, coldness and powerlessness! Many say that there was no real worship until the charismatic movement came along — not for two millennia! Some assert that Christ's people have had their basic spiritual rights and blessings denied them for all these centuries because the wicked clergy, in order to sustain their elitist power and dominance, suppressed the facts about the gifts which should have been exercised and enjoyed by everyone. With such ideas as these, charismatics deride the age of the Spirit as an extended dark age of lifeless formalism. It is claimed that an ugly breach occurred in the spiritual life of God's people, extending from the close of the book of *Acts* until about 1955, when light and power broke forth again in the tongues and visions of charismatic pioneers.

The idea is chilling; the implications staggering. Is the charismatic movement a rediscovery of authentic Christianity? Has the genuine article really been missed by the great instruments of reformation and revival in ages past? Have all the sermons preached and hymns written over a period of 2,000 years been composed in the shadows of an age of spiritual ignorance? Has all the worship of these past years been void of vital life and power? Have numerous lifetimes of devoted labour been sacrificed on the altar of an inadequate and partial faith?

It has been said that the doctrines of the charismatic movement are either *true*, in which case the last 1,900 years have been an age of tragic spiritual deprivation, or these doctrines are *false*, in which case they represent a message of monumental arrogance, decrying the faith and experience of all our spiritual forebears.

There have, we know, been some extremely rare and isolated incidents of phenomena corresponding to present-day charismatic experiences, but these are so few as to be statistically irrelevant in the history of the Church of Christ. However, they are eagerly clutched at by charismatic authors anxious to convince their readers that the 'gifts' of the Spirit have always been manifested. But these writers know perfectly well that their use of history is slick and unethical. They build an Empire State Building out of two or three small bricks, shamelessly misleading their readers with ludicrous exaggerations and generalisations. The incontrovertible fact is that the history of the Church of Christ — the age of the Spirit — has proceeded for the most part without the charismatic movement.

As we have already indicated, it was around 1955 that Pentecostal doctrines began to spread out into other denominations. At first, this occurred extremely slowly, but in April 1960 the rector of an Episcopal church in California announced to his congregation that he had received the baptism of the Spirit and spoken in tongues. This event, which attracted widespread television and newspaper coverage in the USA and gave rise to a best-selling book, is often cited as the effective launching of the modern charismatic movement.

At first, the movement spread rapidly among people with a fairly loose hold on evangelical doctrines, appealing also to many liberals and Catholics. Interestingly, the first crop of societies set up for the promotion of charismatic gifts made it their declared aim to employ the 'gifts of the Spirit' as a means of joining all Christians together in a united Christian front. The overwhelming majority of charismatic leaders still hope for a world-wide ecumenical church under the leadership of the Pope. The charismatic movement has certainly spread extensively within the Roman Catholic Church. However, while vast numbers of priests now employ charismatic jargon and methods of worship, their Catholic doctrines remain totally unchanged. In Third World countries the charismatic movement has seen quite phenomenal expansion, but the kind of churches which have sprung into being often resemble cult meetings much more than Christian churches.

Alongside all the extremism and all the excesses, it must be recognised that the charismatic movement includes many people who are genuine and earnest disciples of the Lord. Equally there are some charismatic fellowships which remain untainted by the worldliness, shallowness, gimmickry and phoney claims which characterise charismatics generally. Nevertheless, even in these better groups, charismatic practices are a great and serious departure from the Bible which will seriously injure true believers, conditioning them for the worse excesses and extremes which are coming in like an irresistible tide.

We cannot be vague or indifferent in our attitude to charismatic claims, and it is hoped that the points raised in this book will help many friends to examine the movement in the light of our only source of guidance for spiritual matters — God's perfect and infallible Word.

1
The Longing for Signs and Wonders

THE 'CHARISMATIC PHENOMENA' which we are witnessing today can be explained by virtue of the widespread scepticism and denial of the Truth in the world around us. God and His attributes and works are denied because of rationalistic, evolutionary, materialistic and atheistic thinking, and in such a world the churches are under tremendous pressure to demonstrate somehow to an unbelieving society that God is alive, that He has power and wisdom, and that He really did do all the mighty miracles and signs which are recorded in His Word.

This is the frame of reference, the atmosphere, which has given rise to the desperate danger we face today, namely the desire to force God to give us (or to conjure up for ourselves) demonstrations of power which will convince ourselves and others that God is indeed the God of Holy Scripture. We have examples in the Bible of times when God's people of old felt a similar desire for a public vindication of their God. The desire was legitimate and worthy, but was never answered by God. Prayers — desperate cries — were made for visible sign-miracles, but they never happened.

An example of this is recorded in *Isaiah 64*. Isaiah was probably the greatest of the writing prophets of the Old Testament, a man who struggled against the scepticism of King Ahaz and against all false worship and occultism (as described in *Isaiah 8*). In his heart, he longed for some visible, genuine, spectacular vindication of the one, true, living God of Israel. Follow his prayer carefully: *Oh, that Thou wouldst rend the heavens and come down, that the mountains might quake at Thy presence — as fire kindles the brushwood, as fire causes water to boil — to make Thy name known to Thine adversaries, that the nations may tremble at Thy presence!*

Was this a legitimate prayer? Of course it was! He wanted his God vindicated before an apostate, sceptical, unbelieving, hard-hearted nation and world. Furthermore, Isaiah had a precedent to quote, for 700 years earlier God had done something like this. So, Isaiah pleaded — *When Thou didst awesome things which we did not expect, Thou didst come down, the mountains quaked at Thy presence* (*Isaiah 64.1-3*).

At the Exodus, and at Sinai, God had publicly vindicated His servant Moses in the eyes of Israel and of Egypt and of all the nations of the world. There had been an absolutely spectacular combination of sign-miracles to such an extent that when Mount Sinai was shaken by the power of God and smoked as a furnace and a great voice was heard, the nation cried out in terror.

Nevertheless, Isaiah's prayer for a new exhibition of God's power went unanswered. He never saw that type of public, spectacular display — apart from the reversal of the shadow on the sundial during the reign of Hezekiah. The Lord knows what He is doing, when He is going to do it, and how He is going to accomplish it. The visible vindication of God is never according to our human desires, suggestions or schemes. It is entirely according to God's sovereign will.

In *Acts 1.6* we read of how the disciples confronted the Lord with this urgent question — *Lord, is it at this time You are restoring the kingdom to Israel*? Our Lord's answer to them echoes to this very hour — *It is not for you to know times or epochs which the Father has fixed by His own authority*. Their task was simply to obey the immediate instructions of the great commission, and to leave the programme, the plan, the chronology, the timing of the introduction of the kingdom and the public vindication of God to Him.

Today we have a situation which is very similar to the desperate cry of Isaiah (later echoed by John the Baptist). It is this — 'Lord, please do something *now!* Look at the state of the churches — look at the decline, look at the humiliation of Thy people today in contrast to the great evidences of blessing in centuries gone by. Do something to vindicate Thy servants, Lord.'

Every major cult and false form of Christianity is offering miracles to its followers in order to vindicate its testimony in an unbelieving world. The rapid growth of cults can be put down to this — the built-in guarantee that people will feel, experience and see visible, public, spectacular vindications of God. So, great and almost irresistible pressure is placed on God's people today to desire some spectacular vindication. Many look at the Bible and say, 'But isn't the Bible just full of sign-miracles? Why is it that people in those days could experience and perform miracles and we cannot?'

The Bible, however, is not 'full' of sign-miracles in the sense of their being continuous. We must never forget that a careful analysis of the Bible shows that miracles did not happen every other week to every other person. They were, in fact, among the rarest events in the history of the world. Any Bible student who takes time to trace through Bible history will discover that

from the time of the creation of the world to the Flood
nearly 1,700 years later, there was only one sign-miracle
recorded, and that was the translation of Enoch without
dying into the presence of the Lord. Of course, in the
final phase of this period there was the ark-building
project, but from outward observation even that was
not a sign-miracle.

From the Flood to the time of the patriarchs, there
was also only one sign-miracle — the judgement of the
Tower of Babel. And from the time of the patriarchs
down to Moses, sign-miracles were very rare. Then,
through four hundred years of bondage in Egypt there
was not one word from Heaven, nor a single sign-
miracle. Suddenly, there came the great outburst of
miraculous signs in the time of Moses and Joshua.
Throughout the crisis of the Exodus and the Conquest
there were many, becoming more spasmodic in the time
of the Judges. Later, the sign-miracles became very rare
once again, and there were none in the time of Solomon.

In the period of the divided monarchy from Solomon
all the way down to Nehemiah, sign-miracles were so
rare as to be practically non-existent. There were, of
course, exceptions. Elijah and Elisha experienced sign-
miracles, and Jonah figured in a great messianic sign.
But set against five centuries, the signs were very few.
Some of the godliest men in that period of history, such
as Ezra, Nehemiah and Zerubbabel, never experienced
one sign-miracle. When the Old Testament period as
such came to a conclusion, there followed a 400-year
period (until the time of John the Baptist) which is
traditionally known as the period of God's silence.
Many interesting things were happening, but there was
not one sign-miracle, and no voice from Heaven.

Even more amazing is the fact that when we come to
John the Baptist, though he was the greatest prophet
that ever lived, the Scripture insists that John never

performed one sign-miracle in his whole life (*John 10.41*). If this is an amazing reflection, what about the Lord Jesus Himself? He was the greatest miracle-worker, and the Son of the living God, yet He did not perform one miracle for the first thirty years of His life.

Some early Christians were so shocked and offended by the statement in *John 2.11* informing us that the changing of water into wine was the first miracle Jesus ever performed, that they foolishly accepted apocryphal Gospels filled with fictional details of sign-miracles which Jesus performed when He was a child and a teenager. They felt a need to fill in the supposed void and to alleviate the intense embarrassment of having the Son of God performing no sign-miracles for thirty years.

Why did the Lord perform no miracle in all those years? It is probably because sign-miracles increase in their value in exact proportion to their rarity. If they had happened constantly and in response to anyone's request or need, they would soon have become commonplace and lost their dynamic, revelatory value. God wisely limited His signs, and so people could not predict when, how or where He would do such things.

Also our God very wisely, and for obvious reasons, eliminated all miracle-working competition from around His beloved Son. Even His own forerunner John the Baptist worked no sign-miracles in order that special attention should be focused on the claims of the Lord Jesus before the nation of Israel. The Old Testament had said over and over again that when the Messiah came, they would know Who He was because of His sign-miracles.

2
Testing Today's Miracles

As we trace through the New Testament we see the precise reason why our Lord Jesus Christ performed His sign-miracles. He did *not* perform spectacular sign-miracles merely in order to demonstrate to Israel that there was a living God in Heaven Who could perform miracles. The Israelites already knew that, because they had been in possession of their Scriptures for hundreds of years and knew all about the character and power of God. That was *not* the reason.

Nor did Jesus perform sign-miracles solely to help people feel better if they were sick, or become whole and healthy if they were crippled. Our Lord explained why He did His miracles. The signs were performed — *that you may believe that Jesus is the Christ, the Son of God*. In *Acts 2.22* the apostles confirmed that Jesus Christ was proved to be the Messiah sent from God by the sign-miracles which He performed.

The Lord Jesus absolutely devastated all charges that He was a false prophet by two things: first, He spoke in accordance with Scripture, in complete harmony with previous revelation; and secondly He made prophecies about sign-miracles that He Himself proceeded to fulfil.

We see the purpose which lay behind our Lord's

miracles in the healing of the paralytic recorded in *Matthew 9.2-8.* As the scene opens, a hopeless cripple is being brought to Jesus by friends. Jesus, seeing their faith, said to the paralytic, *Take courage, My son, your sins are forgiven.* The enemies of Jesus immediately saw this as utter blasphemy. How could a mere, finite, sinful man forgive the sins of another human being? Of course, if Jesus had indeed been finite and sinful, then their opinion would have been correct. But Jesus, knowing their thoughts, said, *Why are you thinking evil in your hearts? For which is easier, to say, 'Your sins are forgiven,' or to say, 'Rise, and walk'?*

If Jesus had *not* truly been the Son of God, the worst possible thing for Him to have done in the presence of a hostile audience would have been to look at a hopeless cripple and say, 'Rise up and walk.' But He did just this, saying — *'In order that you may know that the Son of Man has authority on earth to forgive sins . . . Rise, take up your bed, and go home.' . . . When the multitudes saw this, they were filled with awe, and glorified God.*

The sign-miracle of the instantaneous and perfect healing of the paralytic convinced the multitude that what Jesus had said concerning this man's sins was true — he had been forgiven. The sign-miracle confirmed His power and authority to do the greater thing, namely, to deal with sin. Thus the sign-miracle accomplished *not* a demonstration that God exists; *nor* the helping of a poor cripple; but the sign-miracle chiefly called attention to Christ's unique authority on earth to forgive sin.

We must grasp this essential principle — the message which goes with the sign-miracle is all important. If a sign-miracle ever occurred without having a divine purpose or message attached to it, it would be a total disaster.

It is recorded in *Acts 14* that when Paul and Barnabas

came to the town of Lystra, they found a crippled man outside the city, and they determined in the name of Jesus Christ to heal him. But before they had an opportunity to explain who they were, and Who their God was, the whole city was electrified by the event and rushed out (under the leadership of pagan priests) to offer sacrifices to these two men. The people considered them gods, giving them the names of mythical, pagan gods.

Were Paul and Barnabas pleased to be honoured in this way? No, they rent their garments and cried out in alarm. What went wrong was this: the sign-miracle was not obviously and immediately attached to a message, and so disaster and misunderstanding resulted. This is precisely what is happening today. Hundreds of thousands of professing Christians want sign-miracles in order to vindicate both God and themselves before an unbelieving world. But if there is no supernatural revelation with the signs they become a disaster. A miracle in itself is worse than nothing, unless God, by the miracle, is indicating who the *messenger* is and what the *purpose* really is.

Many of God's people who have a deep desire to honour Him are inclined to believe that He is again speaking in special ways, and certain people are attracting great attention as they perform sign-miracles in support of their messages. By what test can we determine whether they really are receiving new insights directly from God — that is, by means other than the prayerful, careful, systematic study of Scripture?

How can we know whether their so-called sign-miracles are indeed from God or from some other source? We have in the Scripture guide-lines which are very simple and available and which are appropriate for all God's people to use. Using these guide-lines we can obey *1 John 4.1 — Beloved, do not believe every spirit, but test the spirits to see whether they are from God.*

What are these guide-lines? How can we test the miracles of physical healing which every major cult including Roman Catholicism specialises in? How can we determine whether these so-called healings are on the same level and just as genuine as the miracles of healing which we find in the New Testament? Here are three guide-lines from the Scriptures. It is by these 'standards' that we must judge all claims to sign-miracles today:—

(1) The healing miracles of our Lord Jesus Christ were extraordinarily abundant in number.

(2) The healing ministry of our Lord Jesus Christ included *spectacular* healings. They involved dramatic organic and physical restoration which was highly visible and obvious to all.

Now of course, today we have many claims that people have been healed of internal aches and pains, but it is very difficult in most cases for the average person to be sure whether or not a healing has actually taken place. Our Lord specialised in the kind of healing miracle which was obvious and spectacular. For example, in the Garden of Gethsemane the sole contribution of the apostle Peter to the crisis of the hour was to remove an ear from the servant of the high priest. The Lord Jesus picked up the severed ear, put it back in place, and completely healed the wound. Can miracle-workers today achieve the kind of healing that Jesus performed? Of course not.

Jesus was able to heal a man born blind, and the man said, *Since the beginning of time it has never been heard that anyone opened the eyes of a person born blind.* What would happen if one took the body of a loved one who had recently died to a charismatic healer and asked that person to do what Jesus did for Lazarus? We may be sure that no healer would look at such a case and endanger their reputation by attempting to do what they know is altogether impossible. The excuse which 'healers' make today for failing to achieve mighty healings is that the people have no faith, but in the New Testament faith did not necessarily have anything to do with these spectacular healings. Nine out of the ten hopeless lepers whom Jesus healed apparently had no faith. Only one was a believer who came back to thank his Lord. It seems fairly obvious that Lazarus did not need faith to be raised from the dead. So we may be sure that the complaint about smallness of faith in the 'client' is simply a modern excuse, or a cover-up for the fact that these sign-miracles of the Scripture are not being duplicated today.

(3) The most important guide-line of all is this: when the Son of God performed miraculous healings to authenticate His claim to be Israel's Messiah, He did so in such a way *that no one could deny that a miracle of God had taken place.* His sign-miracles were undeniable. Nicodemus came to Him one night and put it this way — *We know that You have come from God as a teacher; for no one can do these signs that You do unless God is with him* (*John 3.2*).

Some of the Lord's enemies who recognised that the miracles were genuine and that people actually were healed and raised from the dead, were forced to conclude that Satan was the one who did all these things. But all were compelled to agree that mighty, spectacular, undeniable miracles occurred. The only debate left was — what supernatural power is the cause, God or the devil?

We read in *John 11.47* that the chief priests and Pharisees gathered in a council and acknowledged that they did not know how to oppose Christ, because He definitely did many miracles. That is echoed in *Acts 4.16* when another Jewish council considered the miracle wrought by Peter and John in healing a paralytic in the Temple. The Jewish leaders said among themselves: *What shall we do with these men? For the fact that a noteworthy miracle has taken place through them is apparent to all who live in Jerusalem, and we cannot deny it.*

Whenever God involves Himself in sign-miracles they are always completely *undeniable*. On Mount Carmel, Elijah, in the name of the true God of Israel, performed a miracle that was totally undeniable. After the fire fell from Heaven, no one asked, 'Did it really happen?' Similarly in Egypt the great plagues leading up to the Exodus forced the magicians to recognise, 'This is the finger of God!'

On the basis of these considerations, I suggest that we have an infallible measuring stick by which to determine whether or not sign-miracles are really happening today. If anyone can observe these miracles and remain sceptical, then they are nothing like the sign-miracles of the Bible and the 'miracle-worker' cannot be from God. This single test demolishes all present-day claims to validity on the part of miracle-workers. God cannot possibly be the author of sign-miracles which can be denied. A comparison of the works of the Lord Jesus and His appointed apostles with the works performed today by charismatic miracle-workers will reveal a stupendous difference. We are looking at two totally different levels of reality.

3
What Are the Greater Works?

THE MODERN TREND of demanding miracles of healing
and claiming to have experienced them, demonstrates a
complete misunderstanding of the key Bible passage in
this whole matter — *John 14.12.* In this passage we
read the promise given by the Lord in the upper room
the night before He died. Once Judas Iscariot had
departed from their midst, leaving eleven true disciples,
the Lord Jesus said these profound words — *Truly,
truly, I say to you, he who believes in Me, the works that I
do shall he do also.*

The eleven disciples did do sign-miracles as Jesus had
done, even raising the dead. But now listen to the
second phase of the promise, and it is this phase which
applies particularly to us — *and greater works than these
shall he do; because I go to the Father.* Think how great
our Lord's works were! They were undeniable and
spectacular. He changed water to wine — an instantaneous performance of a creation-miracle producing a
highly complex biochemical end-product possessing the
appearance of a 'history' it did not have. He multiplied
loaves and fishes, thousands of them, with an appearance of a 'history' not one of them had.

Think of the spectacular healings of hopeless lepers, cripples and blind people. Remember that every one of these sign-miracles had an intentional, God-designed, built-in defect. The water which was changed to wine solved a wedding crisis but it was apparently the last time that such a thing was ever done. No other wedding in Galilee which faced a similar problem would ever receive that kind of help again. In other words, Jesus did not permanently solve that kind of problem in Galilee, and He did not intend to.

Our Lord fed five thousand men on one occasion and four thousand on another. But in so doing, He had no intention of solving the food problem in Galilee. He never planned to. The Lord Jesus healed tens of thousands of people, but we must remember the whole truth about those people whom He healed. Every single one of them died anyway. In other words, He did not permanently solve the problem of their ageing and deterioration. He did not intend to. We may think of poor Lazarus, truly raised from the dead by the Lord Jesus. But when he came back from the dead, he knew he had to die again. He was restored to life with a mortal, sinful body like the one he first died with, because our Lord Jesus did not intend to permanently solve his death problem by that resuscitation.

When we think about these things, we begin to see what our Lord was implying when He said — *Greater works than these shall he do.* There was clearly a work to be done which Jesus did not come to perform personally. His work was to pave the way for a *greater work* by the shedding of His precious blood and His resurrection from the dead. By His atoning death and resurrection He made it possible for us — His disciples — to do the *greater work* which is to take the revelation of God, the true Gospel of Jesus Christ, and to proclaim that message to the ends of the earth.

Every year since the work of Christ was completed thousands of people have heard the Gospel message and by the Spirit of God have believed it. Then a miracle has been performed within their sinful, darkened, spiritually deadened hearts. They have become alive for ever, a miracle which does not have to be repeated; a miracle which is a permanent solution to their every problem. When the Spirit of God entered in to take up His eternal dwelling within their souls, these people became a permanent part of the Body of Christ, eternally forgiven and saved.

Can we deny that this is a far greater work than that of superficial, temporary, physical healings or sign-miracles, great as they undoubtedly were in the physical realm? Miracle healings were only signs; they were never designed by God to be a complete, adequate solution to the real, deep problems of the human race. We see that God's programme for today has a dual purpose:—

(1) Through the *greater works* He is dealing with the spiritual catastrophe of man. Using the faithful, prayerful preaching of the Word of God in local churches, He works through soul-winners and witnessing Christians. This great mission is vastly more important than any claim we may hear about a physical sign-miracle. Such a sign-miracle in this age would be a downward, backward move compared to the greater things now happening through God's people.

(2) God's second purpose is to prepare us for the final phase of His redemptive work. Ultimately He is going to deal with our bodies too. Paul reminds us of God's purpose for these bodies of ours when he says, *Also we ourselves, having the first fruits of the Spirit ... groan within ourselves, waiting eagerly for our adoption as sons, the redemption of our body (Romans 8.23)*. Ultimately God will confirm our spiritual regeneration with a

glorified, physical body when He raises us from the dead, and we become perfect — when we see Him as He is. Then all tears will be wiped away from our eyes, all suffering and pain will cease, all sin will be removed, and we will be in perfection before Him for ever and ever as His servants, having none of the limitations which we now know.

God is preparing us for this, not by giving us instantaneous, spectacular healings to relieve pressure, suffering, inconvenience and discomfort. Today He is preparing us, by His grace, to be those who attract attention to Christ Himself, not to *ourselves* — our claims, our experiences, our healing, our this and that. Let us exhort ourselves and our charismatic acquaintances to focus people upon Christ instead of ourselves. The ultimate tragedy of the charismatic movement is the tremendous emphasis on *me and my experience*, instead of Jesus Christ — His Word, His great commission, His promises, His programme, His timetable, His priorities.

What the churches need desperately today is not some new formula for exorcism, or some new leader for faith-healing. It is not some new wave of tongues-speaking, or some weird serpent or poison ministry. Local churches of Christ need a renewed dedication to the infallible, inerrant, complete, sufficient, written revelation of God in Holy Scripture, preached in the power of the Holy Spirit and out of love for men and women in their lost condition.

4
Today's Gifts
Are Not the Same

WHENEVER ANYONE BECOMES puzzled or confused about the apparent 'gifts' being manifested in the charismatic movement, it is vital to point out that these 'gifts' are nothing like the sign-gifts which were experienced by the apostles and churches of New Testament times. Many Christians (and particularly young believers) seem to accept without question the claim of charismatic teachers that the outbreak of tongues which has occurred in this century is a reproduction of what took place in the first century.

But the kinds of tongues, healings and miracles which we hear about today are altogether different from those of two thousand years ago. In those days speaking in tongues meant speaking in a real foreign language which had not been learned, whereas now it means speaking in a strange, unheard-of language, which is often described as an ecstatic or heavenly language.

As we have already observed, today's healings cannot be compared with the wonderful healing acts of New Testament times either. The healings of those days were instantaneous, organic, and seen by all. Furthermore, no apostle, once he had been moved by God to heal, ever failed to do so. Today, by contrast, healings are claimed for only a tiny proportion of the people who are 'treated' by spiritual healers, and the kinds of conditions that are said to be healed are of a far simpler order than those healed in Bible times.

To defend the present-day kind of tongues-speaking, charismatic teachers maintain that both real and 'spiritual' languages were spoken by tongues-speakers in the early church. To support their teaching they generally refer to *1 Corinthians 13.1* where the apostle Paul uses the expression — *If I speak with the tongues of men and of angels*. This verse, they say, confirms that tongues-speaking may involve heavenly or angelic utterances, but a brief look at the passage shows that this is an obvious mistake of interpretation because Paul is using hyperbole or exaggeration to make a point. He says — *If I speak with the tongues of men and of angels, but do not have love, I have become a noisy gong or a clanging cymbal*. Even if we could do the impossible (that is — speak angels' languages), without love we would be spiritually empty.

Paul uses the same method of argument several times over in these verses. He says, for example, *If I . . . know all mysteries and all knowledge; and if I have all faith, so as to remove mountains, but do not have love, I am nothing*. It should be obvious to us that no Christian will ever know absolutely everything while on earth, nor be able to physically move mountains. It is therefore clear that Paul is using hyperbole to express his point as forcefully as possible.

He draws a picture of a person who has the kind of faith, knowledge and language which is only possible in Heaven, and so he proves that however lofty our spiritual attainments, they are worthless without love. It is very poor interpretation to wrench these words out of their context and to use them in support of the idea that believers on earth may speak angelic tongues.

We know that the tongues spoken in the *Acts of the Apostles* were real foreign languages because foreigners could understand them *(Acts 2.6)*. Eight years later, Peter describes another incident of tongues-speaking as being exactly the same as the incident on the Day of Pentecost *(Acts 11.15-17)*. We also know that the tongues-speaking discussed by Paul in *1 Corinthians* was the speaking of real foreign languages, because Paul says so. In the course of his teaching he explains that all tongues-speaking is a fulfilment of a prophecy by Isaiah, that one day the Jews would be taught by God using foreign lips and strange languages. *Isaiah 28.11-12 is the prophecy.*

It was partly fulfilled when the Babylonians took the Jews into captivity. Through 'foreigners' God chastised His ancient people. But Paul says that the real fulfilment was the sign which God gave in New Testament times. Tongues were therefore real languages — Gentile languages — given as a gift to certain Christians, and designed by God to strike awe into the hearts of doubtful and cynical Jews, and to warn them that He was behind the new church.

Bearing in mind that Luke, the inspired author of *Acts*, and Paul were close companions, it is not possible that they would have used precisely the same term — *tongues* — to describe totally different gifts, one being the ability to speak a foreign language, and the other the inspiration to utter mysterious, extraordinary words, unrelated to normal language. Luke or Paul would never have perpetuated such confusion, and neither would the Holy Spirit of Truth, the divine Author of the Scriptures.

We do occasionally hear today that someone has heard of a case in which a person spoke in a tongue which turned out to be the language of a remote, little-known nation or tribe. But such reports are never substantiated by credible evidence. It is quite certain that no charismatic gathering anywhere today witnesses the amazing phenomenon of believers speaking in real and identifiable foreign languages which they have never learned, like the disciples in Bible times. What passes for a tongue today is usually induced by a little training! There is a technique to be learned in order to get started — but we do not read of this in the Bible.

Most instruction given by charismatic teachers runs along these lines: people are taught that they must stop thinking and praying in their own language. Sometimes they are advised to visualise the Saviour to help them to keep out of normal word-thinking. Then they must lift up their voice in the confidence that God will take the sounds and form them into a divine tongue. If it helps (or so it is commonly taught) then they may repeat certain elementary sounds to themselves. As they begin to utter simple repetitive sounds, a mysterious, ecstatic utterance will emerge.

In New Testament times, however, tongues were real languages which the speakers themselves were able to understand (as we shall see later), and a gift of interpretation was simultaneously given to another person to corroborate the amazing event. This genuine manifestation of the Spirit's power was something which could *never* be counterfeited, and which could stand up to the most cynical scrutiny.

The most 'exclusive' Jew was left confounded, amazed and marvelling whenever the sign was manifested (*Acts 2.6-7*). While it could not produce saving faith, it provided overwhelming evidence of God's power upon the newly-formed Christian church at that time, and it warned that the period of Jewish privilege was at an end. It had a clear and definite message. Such tongues-speaking is not seen anywhere these days.

The charismatic best seller *The Holy Spirit and You* by Dennis and Rita Bennett shows just how far from the New Testament modern tongues-speaking is. In this book Dennis Bennett says that many people have spoken in tongues without even knowing it. He writes that when he tells people about speaking in tongues, someone will occasionally say, 'Oh, you mean that funny little language which I have spoken ever since I was a child, is that it? It makes me feel happy and close to God.'

Mr Bennett speaks of a 'pleasant little Dutch lady' who told him that she had spoken in tongues once and wished she could do so again. When he asked her why she did not try, she replied, 'I wouldn't dare to try! You see, I have a little play language that I talk for my children when we're having fun together and we have a good time, but I'm afraid if I try to speak in tongues, that little play language would come.' Mr Bennett smiled and explained to her that this 'play language' was her tongue. It was what the Holy Spirit had given her.

These writers are among many leading charismatics who believe that the gift of tongues often goes unrecognised. In other words, God's wonderful sign of New Testament times has today turned into such a tiny voice that a charismatic counsellor may have to tell you that you have the gift.

Mr Bennett's total lack of clarity on this subject is also seen when he discusses the question — What are we supposed to feel when we speak in tongues? He tells us: 'At first, you may feel nothing at all; remember this is not an emotional experience. You are trying to let your spirit have freedom to praise God as the Holy Spirit inspires. It may be a little while before your spirit can begin to break through to your feelings, giving you a new awareness of God within you. On the other hand, you may experience a sudden breakthrough, and feel as if you were carried right up into the heavenlies. You will say, "Praise the Lord!" It is wonderful to do that, to become suddenly aware of the fulness of Christ in you and to be carried up by it. Many people just sense a lightness and a reality down in their spirit as they begin to speak.'

While Dennis Bennett says that tongues-speaking is not an emotional experience, he describes it in purely emotional terms. There is nothing here (according to his description) which edifies or touches the understanding, or which speaks a message for others, and so his view of tongues-speaking bears not the slightest resemblance to the experience of New Testament believers. Mr Bennett gives the telling example of a young pastor who was — 'determined to receive the Holy Spirit'. This young man visited Mr Bennett's study where they quietly prayed that he would receive the fulness that he was seeking. Soon he began to tremble very violently and then, 'to speak beautifully in a new language. He continued for perhaps two or three minutes and then stopped.' At this point he looked rather disappointed, thanked Mr Bennett for his help, and left.

The next day he telephoned to say, 'I am really very grateful to you for trying to help me, but you know, I didn't receive anything.' Mr Bennett records that he was on the verge of saying, 'Too bad; better luck next time,' when he felt that that would be foolish. Instead he said, 'Look here, my friend, I saw you tremble under the power of the Holy Spirit and I heard you speak beautifully in a language you do not know. I know you know the Lord Jesus as your Saviour, so this must have been the Holy Spirit. Stop doubting and start thanking the Lord for baptising you in the Holy Spirit.' An hour later the young minister telephoned again to say that he was 'riding high'. He said, 'When you told me to do that, I began to thank the Lord for baptising me in the Spirit and wow, the joy of the Lord hit me and I am now on cloud nine.'

Was this a genuine experience of New Testament tongues? By the standards of the New Testament we can only answer that it was not. The language was not a genuine foreign language; there was no meaning, message, or interpretation; there was no one present who needed the sign-authentication value of the tongue. Therefore there is no reason to believe that this 'ecstatic' utterance was anything different from that spoken in numerous non-Christian cults. Whatever Mr Bennett may think, it was an emotional tongue experienced by a sincere young man who was at the time wrongly convinced that this was God's way, and was very anxious indeed to manifest this strange 'gift'.

Today's gifts, by contrast with those of New Testament times, have absolutely no authenticating quality. Being totally different from the original gifts, they are powerless to confirm that God is uniquely with His people. The apostles and their helpers had gifts which no one could imitate or equal, whereas the tongues and healings performed by charismatic evangelicals today are no different from those which are manifested in the non-Christian religions and cults.

Any number of false religions can do exactly the same things, but many charismatic adherents have no idea of this fact. Tongues-speaking such as we know today is engaged in regularly among Buddhists, Hindus, Mormons, Moslems, Shintoists, spiritists and voodoo devotees. Going back a little in time, many Quakers, the Irvingites, Jansenists and American Shakers, all spoke fluently in unidentifiable tongues just as many evangelicals do today. In recent years many Bible-denying liberals have taken up tongues-speaking, as have very many Roman Catholics, not to mention the extreme 'hippie' and commune groups.

One scholar, writing for a prestigious American sociological institute, found tongues-speaking was practised by the Hudson Bay Eskimos, as well as by the priestesses of jungle tribes in North Borneo. So there is nothing uniquely authenticating in the kind of ecstatic languages spoken today. Any number of cults can do it. Similarly the kind of healing that we get today in evangelical circles is no more effective than the healing ministries carried on by Christian Scientists and so many other non-evangelical organisations. It is not healing of an infallible and uniquely authenticating kind, as in the New Testament.

Indeed, various medical authorities tell us that tongues-speaking is occasionally manifested in connection with certain mental health conditions, such as disassociation, hysteria, epilepsy and schizophrenia. Tongues-speaking has also occurred under the influence of LSD. Obviously, no drug could counterfeit a true spiritual gift. One writer on this subject draws attention to a report by Jung in which he describes a spiritualist medium who spoke in tongues 'fluently, rapidly and with charm. She spoke with bewildering naturalness, and when she had finished there passed over her face an incredible expression of ecstatic blessing.'

Some years ago the newspapers carried a report from the common room of a school in the north of England where the sixth formers had been entertaining themselves by hypnotising one another. On being threatened by the headmaster with expulsion from the school if anyone else was found wandering around in an hypnotic trance, they turned their attention to another mysterious phenomenon. They tried speaking in tongues. None of them were believing Christians, but they managed to speak in tongues very successfully, and did a number of performances for the press.

So between cults, various heretics, the pagan religions of remote tribes, certain health disorders, the sixth-form common room, and charismatic groups, there is nothing uniquely authenticating about tongues-speaking. However, the tongues of New Testament times could never be duplicated by all these people because they were not *ecstatic* languages, but *real ones*. When we consider that tongues-speaking is held up by charismatic teachers as evidence that a person has been baptised in the Spirit, it is a pretty poor kind of evidence, because it can be counterfeited or duplicated by people who are far away from any experience of the Spirit of God.

Today's gifts are therefore completely different from those seen in the New Testament, and because they are not unique to evangelicals they cannot be regarded as being a sign of God to authenticate spiritual experience.

5
The Purpose of
the Gifts Has Changed

BECAUSE THE GIFTS have changed, so that they are no longer astounding, nor unique to the churches of Christ, it is not surprising that new thinking has evolved to clothe them with a new purpose. Charismatic books give entirely different reasons for the gifts from those given in the New Testament. They teach, for example, that the purpose of the gift of tongues is sometimes to bring a message to the assembly of believers, and sometimes for the private worship of God. They also say that it is a special spiritual experience given to believers to strengthen their faith and to bring them closer to the Lord.

Many charismatic writers ask the question, 'Why are people not converted on a massive scale?' And they answer — 'Because we are not doing signs and wonders, and therefore people find it hard to believe. With signs and wonders they would be convinced instantly.' All these ideas, plausible though they may seem, cut across the teaching of the New Testament.

Dealing with tongues first, *1 Corinthians 14.21-22* tells us that their main purpose was to be a sign to unbelieving Jews that God was reproving them and

manifesting His presence to a new church. The gifts
generally were also a sign that a fresh burst of revelation
was going on, that the Messiah had come, and that the
Holy Spirit had come down amidst the church of the
Lord Jesus Christ. Healing gifts had the very special
purpose of giving personal authentication to the apostles as true messengers of God and authors of inspired
Scripture. When people spoke in tongues there was
never any doubt that the Holy Spirit was inspiring the
words. This gift combined the impact of a sign-miracle
with a definite message. When foreigners were present
they were always amazed.

Having wandered far from the scriptural teaching,
and having turned tongues-speaking into a mainly personal experience, charismatic teachers are now in great
confusion about what tongues-speaking really is. The
main writers in the movement contradict each other in
an astonishing way. Some say that tongues-speaking is
God supernaturally communicating with the spirit of
the tongues-speaker, even though the speaker does not
personally understand what the tongue means. Others,
however, say that it is an activity by which the tongues-
speaker communicates with God (again — even though
he does not know what he is saying). In a public
meeting, the interpretation will be God's reply.

Still other charismatic teachers sit on the fence and
say — 'It may be God speaking to you, or it may be you
speaking to God.' One leading writer says: 'The child of
God is privileged to have speech with God, and no man
understands this secret speech for it is the language of
divinity. It is neither understood by the person, nor by
the devil.'

Naturally, if we do not know the meaning of our
words it is difficult to know who is speaking to whom,
let alone what is being said. When the world's leading
charismatic writers have completely opposite ideas of

what tongues-speaking is about, how can anyone feel that they have a biblical warrant for what they are teaching? In New Testament times there was no doubt about the meaning of the foreign languages, and that all tongues-speaking was God speaking to people, and not the other way round. *Then* it was a real and verifiable language supernaturally given. *Now* it is incomprehensible and strange. *Then* it brought a message. *Now* it is used privately without the speaker having any idea what it means. *Then* it was an impressive sign. *Now* it is a strange and disturbing form of unintelligible speech which troubles onlookers and which possesses no solid sign value to authenticate the Gospel.

What about the charismatic argument that signs and wonders should continue today in order to impress unbelievers and bring them to faith in Christ? The short answer is that present-day signs and wonders are simply not up to it, as we have seen already. They do not compare with New Testament signs and healings. Furthermore, even the original signs never actually produced saving faith in the hearts of the onlookers. They certainly proved that the new message was from God, and they also helped to draw in great crowds; but they had no power to promote spiritual faith.

Sometimes the signs and wonders actually hindered the missionary work, because they stimulated a superstitious kind of faith in the crowds (as seen in *Acts 14.11-12*). The purpose of the signs was to authenticate a *new* message, a *new* church, and particularly to authenticate the apostles appointed by the Lord as His true messengers.

Here are some of the scriptures which show that the healing wonders were exclusive to the apostolic band, and that they were intended as signs to authenticate them as true messengers of God:—

And at the hands of the apostles many signs and wonders

were taking place among the people (Acts 5.12).

By word and deed, in the power of signs and wonders, in the power of the Spirit; so that from Jerusalem and round about as far as Illyricum I have fully preached the gospel of Christ (Paul, writing in *Romans 15.18-19*).

The signs of a true apostle were performed among you with all perseverance, by signs and wonders and miracles (2 Corinthians 12.12).

How shall we escape if we neglect so great a salvation? After it was at the first spoken through the Lord, it was confirmed to us by those who heard [the apostles], *God also bearing witness with them, both by signs and wonders and by various miracles and by gifts of the Holy Spirit according to His own will (Hebrews 2.3-4).*

We note that in this last passage the Word of God is already putting the signs and wonders into the past tense. This can only mean that the people were being taught to grasp that signs were already dying out because they had been designed only to give *initial* authentication to the New Testament apostles and the New Testament age. Here in *Hebrews 2* the New Testament is itself beginning to look back and say, 'Don't forget the signs and wonders which authenticated and identified the apostles. Remember how they underlined the fact that they were speaking from God!'

The charismatic movement has made an elementary and grave mistake in assuming that signs and wonders effected by the hands of gifted people were meant to continue down the centuries in order to create and sustain faith. Faith cannot be nourished on the miraculous. Indeed the reverse is true, for if true believers learn to depend on miracles, signs and wonders, then their genuine spiritual faith will soon be weakened and undermined. They will become dependent on these manifestations just as many people in our modern society become dependent on antidepressant drugs. God uses His Word, not signs and wonders, to bring to birth saving faith, and He sustains faith by His personal involvement in the life of the earnest, praying believer.

1 Corinthians 1 is a passage which stands against the idea that signs can create or strengthen faith. After repeating that the teaching of the Cross is the power of God, the apostle says — *For indeed Jews ask for signs, and Greeks search for wisdom; but we preach Christ crucified (vs 22-23).* God does not give the Jews their desired signs (for they would not produce saving faith), nor does He give the Greeks the intellectual flattery which they crave (for that would not stir them to saving faith either). Instead, the presentation of the Gospel will be found to possess all the power of God.

The original purpose of the sign-gifts was to be the divine stamp of authentication upon the first messengers of Calvary and their message. Now that the message has long since been delivered the original purpose has been fulfilled and the sign-gifts have no further role to play. To give them a role, charismatic teachers have had to create new purposes, none of which agree with God's original aims.

6
Is the Word of God Complete?

WHAT IS THE STATUS of the Word of God? Is it complete or not? Is it really *the faith which was once for all delivered*, or is it still in the process of being revealed to us? The most serious error of the charismatic movement is that its ideas about prophecy and miracles strike at the very foundation of the Scripture as a completed revelation. Many sincere believers in God's Word have been drawn into charismatic ideas without realising that this teaching undermines the total authority of the Scripture.

According to the charismatic view, prophecy is still going on. According to the Bible, all revelation was completed in the time of the apostles and no further direct revelation of authoritative Truth is to be expected. Here are the passages in John's Gospel in which the Lord Jesus emphasised that the disciples would be led by the Holy Spirit to deliver ALL the Truth, so as to give a COMPLETE, perfect, and finished revelation.

But the Helper, the Holy Spirit, whom the Father will send in My name, He will teach you all things, and bring to your remembrance all that I said to you (John 14.26).

When the Helper comes, whom I will send to you from

the Father, that is the Spirit of truth, who proceeds from the Father, He will bear witness of Me, and you will bear witness also, because you have been with Me from the beginning (John 15.26-27).

I have many more things to say to you, but you cannot bear them now. But when He, the Spirit of truth, comes, He will guide you into all the truth; for He will not speak on His own initiative, but whatever He hears, He will speak; and He will disclose to you what is to come. He shall glorify Me; for He shall take of Mine, and shall disclose it to you (John 16.12-14).

Scripture is complete, and we are given a trust to keep it that way in the letter of *Jude: I felt the necessity to write to you appealing that you contend earnestly for the faith which was once for all delivered to the saints (Jude 3).* As we are taught in the closing verses of *Revelation,* there will be no further revelation. The vision and the prophecy is now sealed up.

Charismatic author J. Rodman Williams writes in a manner which is typical of so many charismatic authors when he insists that God is still speaking through tongues and prophecies. In his book, *The Era of the Spirit,* he writes: 'In prophecy God speaks. It is as simple, and profound, and startling as that! What happens in the fellowship is that the word may suddenly be spoken by anyone present, and so variously, a "Thus says the Lord" breaks forth. Most of us, of course, were familiar with prophetic utterances as recorded in the Bible, and willing to accept it as the Word of God. Isaiah's or Jeremiah's "Thus says the Lord" we were accustomed to, but to hear a Tom or a Mary today . . . speak the same way! Many of us had convinced ourselves that prophecy ended with the New Testament . . . until suddenly through the dynamic thrust of the Holy Spirit, prophecy comes alive again.'

Charismatic teachers protest that their prophecies,

visions and 'words of knowledge', though direct messages from God, do not undermine Scripture because all
of them must be tested by the Scriptures. But the
simple fact is that countless prophecies and visions
'received' by charismatic believers are not tested by the
Bible, and vast numbers of revelations are received
which *cannot* be so tested because they are about current
affairs in the believer's church or circle. How can a
message be tested when it simply accuses someone of
insincerity, or declares that someone will recover from a
very ordinary illness?

Even where modern prophecies are simply restate-
ments of biblical Truth, they undermine the Scripture,
for God has said that the Bible is the sole vehicle of
revelation, and it is completely sufficient for all our
needs. God has said that there will be no more Truth
revealed by direct messages or voices on occasions when
we need guidance, comfort or encouragement. We will
not be provided with extra revelation of any kind, for
we are to use the doctrines, promises and comforts
already revealed in the Scripture to guide us in every
case.

It is not good enough for charismatic teachers to say
that their 'extra' messages do not actually contradict the
Bible. They certainly undermine it in another way —
they provide an alternative fountain of light and help,
and they train the people of God away from the one
source of objective Truth. The Lord has spoken to us
clearly through Paul in *Romans 15.4 — For whatever
was written in earlier times was written for our instruction,
that through perseverance and the encouragement of the
Scriptures we might have hope.*

The fact is that charismatic teachers do not grasp that
the Scriptures are (a) complete, (b) totally sufficient for
all our needs, and (c) deep and profound enough for
every possible problem and situation. Whether they

have done it consciously or not, they have joined the ranks of heretics in their downgrading of the Word of God. The Roman Catholic Church has added to the Bible by trusting her own church traditions and leaders as authoritative. Liberal theologians have placed their reason and the science of the day on a par with Scripture. Heretical 'pietistic' movements have put their own 'inner light' on the same level as Scripture — and that is exactly what countless charismatic leaders do to an ever increasing extent.

The Scriptures are complete, and, as the *Baptist Confession of Faith* of 1689 puts it, 'Nothing at any time is to be added whether by new revelation of the Spirit, or tradition of men.' Neither must we add to it or supplement it by prophecies, tongues, interpretations, visions or experiences.

The completing of the New Testament was part of the 'foundation stage' of the Church, and special revelational gifts (apostles and prophets) were given to the Church for this period. Once the Word of God was complete the foundation stage was over, and the revelational gifts were no longer given. Consider for a moment the biblical picture of a foundation stage.

The apostles performed sign-miracles in order to establish that the Messiah had come, and had revealed His Word to them. Thus, in *Ephesians 2.19-20* we read — *So then you are no longer strangers and aliens, but you are fellow citizens with the saints, and are of God's household, having been built upon the foundation of the apostles and prophets, Christ Jesus Himself being the corner stone.*

We note that the Church is built, not on the foundation of Jesus Christ, but on the *foundation of the apostles and prophets*. Of course, Christ is the true foundation of the Church, for *no man can lay a foundation other than the one which is laid, which is Jesus Christ;* but another foundation — the apostles and prophets — is necessary for one very good reason. Let us remember that Jesus Christ, Who died as our substitute, and is the Author of our faith, did not write one word of the Bible. And we would never know anything of what He did on that cross, nor would we have heard of the empty tomb and the resurrection but for the function uniquely performed by the apostles and prophets. From a revelatory standpoint, all we know about God and His beloved Son and the true Gospel comes uniquely through the apostles and prophets of Bible times.

The Lord Jesus is the chief corner-stone, but apostles and prophets wrote the entire New Testament. Two apostles and two prophets wrote the four Gospels; the two apostles were Matthew and John and the two prophets were Mark and Luke. What is the difference between these two kinds of inspired person? The apostles were men who were chosen by God to walk with Jesus in His public ministry for three and a half years and, in the case of some of them, to have special revelation to write Scripture. Prophets were men who had not necessarily walked with Jesus, but who also received messages from God, and some received special revelation to write Scripture.

The whole of the New Testament was written by apostles and prophets. There were apostles such as Peter, John and the special apostle Paul, and prophets such as Luke (who wrote *Acts*) and James and Jude, half-brothers of Jesus, plus the author of *Hebrews*. The Lord Jesus did not write one word. This group of apostles and prophets is a limited, special, chosen group that constituted the revelatory foundation of the Church in Holy Scripture. There can be no more of them for they are the foundation. A building can have only one foundation, and this must be fixed, stable, complete and secure before the building is erected. Therefore, there can be no other apostles and prophets besides those who are called in Scripture — *the foundation*.

Paul was a special apostle prepared by God to provide a bridge from the Israelite apostles who walked with Jesus, to the Gentile world. In *1 Corinthians 15* Paul says that the risen Lord Jesus was seen by all the apostles — *and last of all he was seen of me also, as of one born out of due time (AV)*. Paul indicates here that he was the last apostle — there were no more.

Today, the complete and finished character of revelation is disliked by many Christians. The attitude of people in the charismatic and similar movements today runs something like this: 'This is unfair! I want to be a prophet. Why did God only teach through them? I have equal, if not greater faith. I want to be a channel of new revelation; I want to be a spokesman, a voice, a mouthpiece for God. I want divine words to come from my tongue.'

The only biblical response to such an attitude is to say — 'You may not have that privilege. You have not been specially chosen by God to be part of the foundation of His Church. The foundation is long since finished. You are now in the superstructure phase of church history. You can never have special revelatory privileges. It has nothing to do with whether God has the power to do it, or whether you have the faith to receive it. It is all to do with the fact that God has not planned that His Church should have 14, 15 or 20 different foundations, or 75 or 156 different apostles and prophets. There are no more apostles and prophets.'

How thrilled and thankful we should be for the privileges which our God has given us. We should not want or demand illegitimate privileges. We should not want to twist and misrepresent His Truth in order to have experiences which God never intended us to have in this phase of the history of His Church.

Even within the lifetime of the apostles — as the

completion of the Scriptures drew near — there are indications that their power to work sign-miracles was being withdrawn. Take the example of Paul. It would appear that the last sign-miracle of healing he ever experienced was when he cast off a deadly poisonous serpent on the island of Malta. That occurrence astonished the inhabitants of that small island and attracted attention to Paul's divine authority as an apostle. As far as we can tell, however, it was his last healing experience, because he subsequently wrote letters which included statements like these:—

First, to Philippi, his favourite church: 'Thank you for your generous gift through Epaphroditus. How sorry he is to learn that you have heard of his illness. But thank God, God has had mercy upon us and raised him up.' Now this illness of Epaphroditus was a very long one, yet there is not one hint that Paul healed him. How could his illness have been prolonged if Paul had still possessed the power of instantaneous, supernatural healing?

And then Paul wrote in his last letter, *2 Timothy*, these words; *Trophimus I left sick at Miletus*. Why did he do that? If he had the power to heal him, why did he not do so? The implication is that he could not heal him. In fact Paul said to Timothy: 'For your frequent ailments and for your stomach's sake, change your diet from unsafe water to some fruit juice.'

Do we understand what this implies? The foundation of the Church was now in the final stages of completion. Some have suggested that by the time AD 70 arrived, which Paul never lived to see, the whole problem of tension with Israel ended with the destruction of the Temple, and so the sign-miracles of the apostolic era ended.

Whether or not this was the precise moment of their withdrawal, Paul did not have to wait until AD 70.

He experienced, as it were, the scaffolding of the foundation of the Church being removed. As the inscripturated revelation upon which the Church of Christ would be built drew to completion, the signs abated. It is entirely probable that John, the last survivor of the apostles, never experienced in his later life any more sign-miracles of healing.

Because we have the Saviour's express words to the effect that *all* the Truth would be committed to the disciples, and because the revelatory gifts are described by Paul as foundational, we must never add to, or subtract from the Word of God as it stands revealed. *Every word of God is tested,* says *Proverbs 30.5-6 — Do not add to His words lest He reprove you, and you be proved a liar.*

If we add anything to what God has said, He will add to us the plagues which He has written in the book of *Revelation,* as we are warned in the last verses of the Bible. These plagues are described in *Revelation 6* to *19.* Therefore, we must want to be very careful to know the boundary lines of God's revealed Word. He is not interested in our additions, or our adjustments, or our revisions of His revelation of Truth.

This Word is infinitely important, precious, valuable material and God says to us, as He did to Israel — 'Do not dare add one word to what I have said, because if you do, you will be under judgement.' That is what we must weigh, as we think of the place of 'prophecy' today. What are we doing to God's foundation — to God's apostolic and prophetic revelation? How does the idea that God is inspiring prophets today affect the uniqueness and significance of what God has said in His Word? It destroys that uniqueness, and steals from the exclusive and absolute authority of God's perfect and only Word.

7
Tongues Were Never for Personal Benefit

NOWADAYS, THE PRACTICE of tongues-speaking is
encouraged in charismatic circles largely for personal
benefit. It is desired as a *personal* sign, and for its
spiritual, emotional and ecstatic value in private devotions. But this is due to a failure to grasp the plain
teaching of the New Testament that *all* the gifts were
designed to benefit the whole church. They were never
intended for the subjective and personal benefit of the
tongues-speaker. *1 Corinthians 12.7* makes this clear to
us — *But to each one is given the manifestation of the
Spirit for the common good.* ('The common good' is a
phrase also employed by the *NIV.* The *MLB* says 'the
common welfare'. The *NKJV* says that the gifts were
given 'for the profit of all'.)

The principle should be clear — each gift is given to
benefit in some way the *whole church*, not the individual
who possesses the gift, and furthermore Paul has in
mind not a local church but the church at large.
Apostles, for example, were not present in the vast
majority of local churches, but their inspired teaching
benefited all the churches.

Because tongues-speaking was a sign to Jews, it

validated the new Christian church for Jewish people
and therefore it was an enormous benefit to the whole
church. In addition, of course, the actual message
which came via a tongues-speaker was a 'prophecy'
which benefited the congregation which heard it. It was
certainly a rather cumbersome form of prophecy, for it
required translation, and for this reason it was inferior
to straightforward prophecy. The sign value of the
foreign-tongue method of prophecy inevitably detracted
from its efficiency. Nevertheless, the message which
came via the tongue was a real word from God to
the assembled believers, and the tongues-speaker was
therefore a type of prophet. Where, then, do charismatic teachers find their authority for the 'private' use of
tongues in prayer or personal devotions? The answer,
amazing as it may seem, is that they take their authority
from verses which are meant to show that tongues must
not be used in this way.

One such verse is *1 Corinthians 14.2 — For one who
speaks in a tongue does not speak to men, but to God.*
Tongues-speaking occurred when the Holy Spirit
moved men to speak, as we see from all the references in
Acts. God gave the words, and therefore tongues were a
message from God to the people, and not the other way
round.

The tongues-speaker of *1 Corinthians 14.2* clearly has
a message from God which he understands, for Paul
goes on to say that he edifies himself. It would therefore
appear that Corinthian tongues-speakers were not
troubling to translate their utterances into everyday
language, and so the apostle shows them the absurdity
of their omission. If God gives the messages in the first
place, he argues, and the tongues-speaker (or interpreter) fails to translate them for the church, then God
Himself ends up as the only listener!

Such a situation is preposterous because it turns the

whole purpose of tongues-speaking on its head. Tongues — declares Paul — are not for God's benefit, or for the benefit of the individual tongues-speaker, but they are words from God intended to be heard and understood in the public gathering of the church. Here was the acid test for all tongues-speaking in those days — did it bring a message from God to the church? The tongues-speaker *must* interpret so that the church may be edified (see *1 Corinthians 14.5*).

Charismatic teachers use *1 Corinthians 14.4* to support the idea of private tongues-speaking — *One who speaks in a tongue edifies himself*. However, Paul is not justifying 'selfish' tongues-speaking, but dealing with the great mistake of failing to translate the tongue for the rest of the congregation. Throughout his statement he says repeatedly that tongues *must* yield a message for the assembly. Says Paul — 'Whoever speaks a foreign-language message without providing an interpretation speaks to himself, edifies himself alone, and so misuses the message which he has been given.' The fact that these tongues-speakers were *edified* (which means that their *understanding* was built up) tells us that they definitely understood the meaning of their tongues themselves. Perhaps for some of them the demonstration of the gift had become more important than its purpose.

When the New Testament declares that all tongues-speaking must *edify*, it disqualifies any uninterpreted tongue which does not lead to the upbuilding of the *understanding*. This means that it is not possible to have the gift of tongues simply as an emotional-cum-spiritual experience. Whenever the word translated *edify* (meaning — to build up) is used in the Greek New Testament it is used in a context which has to do with learning some tangible truth, dispelling all mystery, superstition or confusion. Edification may be accomplished by words of instruction, encouragement or testimony, or even by the power of example, but in every case a definite and describable lesson is received by those who benefit, so that their understanding is built up. Beyond all controversy it means — to build up the understanding. (See *Romans 14.19; 15.2; 1 Corinthians 8.1; 10.23; 14.3* and *12; 2 Corinthians 10.8; 12.19; 13.10; Ephesians 4.12-16; 1 Thessalonians 5.11; 1 Timothy 1.4-5.*)

Charismatic teachers think that in *1 Corinthians 14.13-14* Paul sanctions the idea that one may speak in a tongue without understanding it — *Therefore let one who speaks in a tongue pray that he may interpret. For if I pray in a tongue, my spirit prays, but my mind is unfruitful.* To charismatic believers these words teach that one may pray in tongues (in spirit) even though the understanding is blank. But this is out of the question for the believer, because the *mind* is always involved in spiritual activities. Paul says most emphatically — *I shall pray with the spirit and I shall pray with the mind also (1 Corinthians 14.15).*

How, then, do we account for the fact that a Corinthian tongues-speaker may find himself in a position where he has a tongues message which he does not understand? It is likely that the apostle's words deal with the case of a gifted tongues-speaker whose message fails to come. Let us suppose that the speaker has been given the gift of foreign-language utterance many times before. One day, in the course of public worship, while filled with love and praise to God, he feels a strong inclination to 'give utterance' in his Spirit-given language. Perhaps the foreign-language words take shape in his mind, but on this occasion the words are not accompanied by any understanding of what they mean. (Someone who often spoke in tongues would doubtless remember many words or phrases of his language(s), and when filled with a strong desire to be used by God to bring a message to the congregation, some of these phrases may have involuntarily crowded into his consciousness.)

If he is given no understanding of the meaning of the words, the tongues-speaker is evidently not under the moving of the Spirit, because tongues-speaking — like praying and singing — must involve the understanding. Though the foreign words jostle in his mind, straining to be 'set free', they have no form or meaning because the Lord is not giving him a message for this particular meeting. In these circumstances he must not speak out. The command of the apostle to a tongues-speaker in this predicament is (we paraphrase freely) to pray for an utterance which carries a clear message with it (*1 Corinthians 14.13*).

There is yet another verse in *1 Corinthians 14* which charismatic teachers use to show that people may speak and pray in tongues privately — *But if there is no interpreter, let him keep silent in the church; and let him speak to himself and to God* (*v 28*).

As any careful reader will realise, the apostle cannot be sanctioning the private use of tongues-speaking. He would never contradict his earlier statements that tongues are (a) for the benefit of the whole church, (b) are useless unless they are interpreted, and (c) are intended to be a public sign to create awe in the hearts of Jewish observers. The charismatic interpretation of this verse forces Paul to sweep away everything he has previously said about tongues-speaking!

In this verse Paul deals with a further possibility which may occur in the worship of the church at Corinth when a tongues-speaker rises to give his message. We may suppose that this speaker is in a different situation from that of the previous case who did not understand the words which came into his mind. This speaker apparently understands them and believes he has a genuine message from God. However, Paul insists that he must still consult with his fellow tongues-speakers to see if one of them is able to understand and interpret his tongue.

Thus God provides a double-check on all tongues-speaking. First, the speaker must understand his tongue himself and then an interpreter must confirm that the same sense has been given to him also. This provision completely eliminates the possibility that a tongues-speaker may be mistaken and imagine a meaning for his tongue; after all, even a godly man may well get carried away and make such a mistake. This 'dual-interpretation' arrangement confirmed to the sceptical Jewish outsiders that the gift was an undeniable miracle — we remember that the chief value of tongues-speaking was as a sign to the Jews.

The practical matter of how the tongues-speakers collaborated is probably explained in *1 Corinthians 14.28-30*, where we are given the impression that all the prophets (which probably included the tongues-speakers) sat together. There would not have been many of them (if we remember the small number of prophets at Antioch — *Acts 13.1*) and they would have been able to consult easily before or during the meeting.

If no interpreter is inspired to corroborate a tongue, then the speaker is commanded to speak to himself, and to God, which does not mean that he promptly engages in private tongues-speaking in the assembly! It simply means that he is to keep his words to himself and pray to God to clear his mind and use him another time, in His sovereign will and pleasure. In other words, he holds his peace and submits to the overruling will of God. Perhaps he silently 'hears out' his message for sharing with the teachers and prophets later, but he is not authorised to speak it audibly in the absence of an inspired interpreter. The sum of Paul's teaching here is that all genuine tongues are a message to the congregation. Their meaning will be understood by the speaker and confirmed by an interpreter.

If ever these requirements cannot be met, then the tongues-speaker must be silent and pray to God for leading. The private use of tongues is therefore precluded by the apostle, who insists that all spiritual gifts must result in the edification of the church and the provision of a truly supernatural sign to Jewish people. Nevertheless, charismatic teachers use these verses as a licence for private and mystical tongues-speaking.

8
Should We Personally Seek the Gifts?

THE APOSTLE PAUL'S exhortation to *earnestly desire the greater gifts* (*1 Corinthians 12.31*) is used by charismatic teachers to prove that all believers should aim at exhibiting charismatic gifts, but this is a most superficial interpretation of the verse. Two questions must be asked as we read this verse — who is the apostle speaking to? And, what are the greater gifts? In answer to the first question, the apostle is not speaking to *individuals*, but to the *entire Corinthian church*.

It is the *local church* as a whole which is to earnestly desire the greater gifts, and to pray for and value them. For an *individual* to be ambitious for gifts would be wrong, but for the church to desire them is right. If Paul means that *individuals* should desire to have the greater gifts for themselves, then we are all commanded to nourish the ambition of being apostles, which is clearly wrong.

What is the greatest gift? Is it tongues-speaking? Is it healing? The answer is given in *1 Corinthians 12.28*; the greatest gift is *apostleship*, and the least gift is *tongues*. In other words Paul tells us (as congregations) not to desire or covet after tongues, but to desire apostleship. But how can the church earnestly desire the gift of apostleship? The answer lies in the Greek word *zeloo* which is translated *earnestly desire* (*covet* in the *AV*). This word means: to be zealous for something. (Our English word *zeal* comes from the Greek — *zelo*.) Paul means that we are to be warmly in favour of apostles. We are to strongly support them.

Earnestly desiring the gift of apostleship means that the church will zealously heed and value the teaching of existing apostles. It does not mean that the church must desire *more* apostles. Churches are also commanded to appreciate and desire the other teaching ministries which God gives, praying for pastors and teachers and appreciating the faithful exposition of the Word.

Where, then, does the teaching come from that we must all covet and desire to speak in tongues? It comes from a simple misreading of Paul's words.

In *1 Corinthians 14.39*, the apostle tells the Corinthians — *desire earnestly to prophesy* — which also means that they must zealously and gratefully appreciate the temporary ministry of the prophets (who were given by God until the Scripture was complete). He does not tell individual church members to be ambitious to prophesy, but he exhorts the church as a whole to desire and value prophets. The charismatic view of this verse is that each believer should long to prophesy, but this idea is contrary to the biblical teaching that spiritual gifts are dispensed solely according to the sovereign will of God (*1 Corinthians 12.7-11*). The apostle tells us very firmly that they are distributed comparatively sparingly (*1 Corinthians 12.29-30*) and not on the basis of spiritual ambition.

The command to earnestly desire the greater gifts, therefore, is made to churches, not individuals. And even if it was a command to individuals, it would not justify a believer being ambitious to speak in a tongue, for that is listed by the apostle as the *least gift*, not the greatest. While tongues-speaking had a powerful 'verification value' in its day, Paul placed it far below direct prophecy, and even below the ordinary teaching ministry. He placed it bottom of his list of spiritual gifts in *1 Corinthians 12.28*, and he did not mention tongues at all in other lists of gifts such as those in *Romans 12* and *Ephesians 4*. Yet today, thousands crave for this least gift.

Charismatic teachers nearly all insist that after conversion Christians must seek the baptism of the Holy Spirit as a separate experience, and that when they receive this baptism it will be marked by their speaking in tongues. Therefore tongues are earnestly desired by many believers who long for evidence that they have received the Spirit. Tongues are thus no longer a sign to Jews, or a message for the congregation, but a sign of a personal spiritual experience.

While it is a praiseworthy thing to desire more spiritual life, the idea that a born-again Christian needs a separate baptism of the Spirit stems from two basic mistakes in understanding God's Word. The first mistake is to confuse two entirely different experiences of the Holy Spirit — the *baptism* of the Spirit, and the *filling* of the Spirit. According to *1 Corinthians 12.13* all true Christians (without exception) are baptised by the Spirit at conversion when the Holy Spirit brings them into the family of the redeemed. However, believers may and must be *filled* with the Spirit repeatedly, as we see from a study of the 'fillings' in *Acts*. We are commanded in *Ephesians 5.18* to constantly seek the *filling* of the Spirit.

This *filling* of the Spirit is an infinitely repeatable bestowal of power upon believers, though Scripture does not indicate anywhere that there are any 'feelings' associated with it. It is a practical blessing given when we need boldness, fluency and clarity in our witness, dedication for service, and help to conquer our sins. The rule of Scripture is — one baptism, many fillings — and the references to repeated fillings in *Acts* and *Ephesians* show that they were not generally attended by tongues-speaking.

At the end of this chapter we list many texts which show that the baptism of the Spirit takes place at conversion, proving that the principal plank of charismatic thinking is therefore totally misguided.

The second mistake which leads to the idea that believers must seek a baptism of the Spirit (marked by the gift of tongues) arises from a serious misunderstanding of what took place on the Day of Pentecost. It is imagined that all believers must have their own personal 'Pentecost' following their conversion. But on the Day of Pentecost the Spirit of God came down in power on the New Testament church in a 'once only' event (like the incarnation or the atonement). It signalled the end of the Jewish church during which a minority of truly converted Israelites were obliged to worship in a State church peopled and run by those who were unregenerate.

At Pentecost God changed everything (as He had long promised He would), inaugurating the New Testament church with a fresh burst of revelation, accompanied by signs and wonders. This new church was *separate*, *spiritual*, *international*, composed of regenerate souls, and under the direct rule of the Holy Spirit of God. Once the Spirit of God came down to form and to rule the New Testament church, He never withdrew. Pentecost was a unique and unrepeatable baptism of the Spirit upon the church.

At Pentecost the disciples were all 'baptised' by the Spirit into one body — the true Church of Christ; but since then each individual convert is 'baptised' by the

Spirit into the true Church of Christ at the time of conversion, as Paul tells us in *1 Corinthians 12.13* — *For by one Spirit we were all baptized into one body, whether Jews or Greeks, whether slaves or free, and we were all made to drink of one Spirit*. Therefore, the instant a person is converted he is baptised into the invisible Church, and he may be certain that the Spirit is within him. Agonising and emotional seeking for the baptism of the Spirit is therefore completely misplaced, for He is already within the true believer. As Paul says, *If anyone does not have the Spirit of Christ, he does not belong to Him (Romans 8.9)*.

In charismatic circles the primary purpose of any gift of the Spirit is to give signs, wonders and private ecstatic pleasure. Indeed, these things have assumed a greater importance than the *fruit* of the Spirit in the life of the believer. The sign-gifts which authenticated the bearers of new Scripture and ushered in the church age have ceased, and it is the fruit of the Spirit which continues to be produced in the lives of Christ's people.

The filling of God's Spirit is not given, as charismatic teachers claim, for private, ecstatic pleasure, or as a sign, but for practical purposes. We have already noted that the *fillings* recorded in *Acts* gave the disciples boldness, fluency, love and real dedication to the work of God. In *Ephesians 5* we are exhorted to be filled with the Spirit for righteousness and holiness. One of the ways in which we bear fruit is that we grow in Christian character, even though we may pass through valleys of hardship, persecution, sorrow and affliction. But charismatic teachers advocate signs, wonders and ecstatic experiences as a means of floating across such valleys.

The Bible teaches that the Lord will often withdraw His smile and permit trials to come upon us, for a variety of reasons. Sometimes we may have to be chastised for sin or disobedience, and sometimes experience trials or sickness in order that we may be taught the ugliness of this vain world, and learn to appreciate the Lord and His wonderful ways. Many times we shall be taken through hard experiences to wean us from worldly tastes, or to train up some special quality in us, such as patience or sensitivity.

The Lord has much to do in our lives, but if we depend upon the artificial crutches of supposed signs and wonders, believing that trials and sicknesses are not God's will for us, then the real fruits of patience and holiness will never be manifested in us. The charismatic use of ecstatic experiences insulates believers from reality, but true biblical teaching enables believers to view all their trials and circumstances spiritually, and to manifest the fruit of Christian character and dependence upon God in them all. The purpose of God for His people is not that they should permanently manifest sign-ministries, but that they should be perfected in holiness to become a wholesome, righteous people, walking in genuine patience and trust.

Scripture texts which prove that the believer is baptised with the Holy Spirit at the time of conversion include the following:
John 7.37-39; Acts 2.38; Romans 5.1-5; Romans 8.9 and *15; 1 Corinthians 6.11* and *19-20; 1 Corinthians 12.13; Galatians 3.2* and *5; Galatians 4.4-6; Ephesians 1.13-14; Ephesians 4.30; 1 Thessalonians 1.5-6; 1 John 4.12-13.*

9
Bypassing the Mind and the Word

WHAT HARM CAN CHARISMATIC practices do to evangelical believers who take them up? Among the injuries which they will suffer is the undermining of spiritual faculties, especially the priceless faculty of spiritual discernment and *understanding*. We have already seen that all spiritual gifts must *edify* — a word which the Greek New Testament always uses to indicate the building up of our understanding. All gifts *must instruct the mind*. Every word in the Bible is directed at the conscience, affections and will of the believer *through the mind*, and so important is the centrality of our reasoning faculty that Paul tells Timothy that God has given us the *spirit of . . . a sound mind* (*2 Timothy 1.7, AV*).

We must always respond to God in accordance with the Saviour's principle for worship — *in spirit and truth* (*John 4.24*). All prayer and worship is to be understood by our rational minds and directed to God as a voluntary, conscious act. The mind is never to be left out. Paul says (*1 Corinthians 14.5*) that we must pray with the spirit and *with the mind also*. We must sing with the spirit and *with the mind also*. (The *AV* renders this: *with the understanding also*).

Contrary to all this is the charismatic idea of tongues, prophecies and visions, where it is obvious that the understanding is bypassed, and the conscious control of words and thoughts is forfeited. Intelligent understanding of the meaning of a privately indulged tongue, for example, is unnecessary. According to charismatic teaching the highest evidences of a believer's communion with God are ecstatic experiences which may bypass the mind altogether, and are felt only at the emotional level.

Although charismatic teachers insist that tongues-speaking and ecstatic worship are not merely emotional experiences, it is beyond argument that things happen which the worshipper does not understand, and which do not build up his knowledge of the Word of God in the least. Therefore, tested by Scripture, most charismatic worship is not in accordance with God's will for true worship or spiritual edification, because all true worship and ministry must be *in spirit and truth*. It must be *in spirit* rather than purely touching the emotions, and *in truth* because it is conducted strictly in accordance with God's revealed pattern. All ministry must be intelligible and understandable, and it must proceed via the mind to touch the heart.

The emotional high or 'cloud nine' experience of many charismatic worshippers is not spiritual, but carnal, because it affects the emotions without instructing the mind. In *Ephesians 5.18* Paul says: *Do not get drunk with wine, for that is dissipation, but be filled with the Spirit.* Being *filled with the Spirit* is the exact opposite of being drunk. When drunk, people lose their minds, because reason and understanding become befuddled, but when filled with the Spirit the mind becomes more alive than ever, and God's Truth is wonderfully grasped and felt. The understanding is enlarged and emancipated. When musing alone, or when doing some menial task which requires no great concentration, Christians may rejoice and worship, singing and making melody in their hearts to the Lord, with psalms and hymns and spiritual songs *(Ephesians 5.19)*, because being filled with the Spirit leads — not to unintelligible languages and ecstasies — but to rational thought and reflection on the things of God.

In *Galatians 5.22* the apostle sets out the *fruit* of the Spirit. Is the mind or understanding bypassed here? Not at all, because every single virtue and Christian practice requires the participation of the mind as well as the heart. One of the virtues listed is *temperance*, or self-control. A believer must never be out of control; never in a 'drunken' ecstasy. Nor may a believer get into any kind of cultish trance-state. A worldling may wish to dull the mental faculties, escape from reality and allow the 'animal' part to enjoy itself, but the Christian, by the help of God, is to grow in understanding and self-control.

The evangelical who becomes charismatic pushes the mind down into an inferior place, and gradually becomes an emotional and subjective kind of person. He now assesses things in an entirely subjective way, rather than in an objective and biblical way. For this person, Scripture loses its total authority and becomes nothing more than a rag-bag of texts taken out of their context and used to prop up charismatic ideas. The charismatic believer moves inevitably (though often without realising it) away from obedience to God's Word, while he places ever increasing trust in anecdotes of strange, emotional experiences and apparent signs and wonders.

Another example of the abdication of proper mental control in charismatic circles is the increasing use of hypnotic techniques. The widespread occurrence of people being 'slain in the Spirit' is an example, and so is the placing of people into trances. This kind of thing used to be the stock-in-trade of the theatrical hypnotist. The performing hypnotist was introduced to the theatre audience as having remarkable powers of hypnosis. The audience hardly needed to be told, for they were familiar with the claims of the billboards outside. In an atmosphere of expectation and 'belief', the hypnotist proceeded to tell the audience — in detail — of the phenomena they were about to witness. The audience did not realise it, but they had already succumbed to the power of hypnotic suggestion by believing that these things would indeed happen. Even cynically-minded people were gripped by a degree of mounting tension and anticipation — in other words their unbelief was tinged with expectation also!

Soon the hypnotist called for volunteers to join him on the platform, and after an impressive display of theatrical-cum-hypnotic mumbo-jumbo, he would 'command' people to display the effects which he had previously said would take place. Some would fall down at a touch; others would be unable to move; a number would find an arm anaesthetised, and so on.

The writer of this chapter recalls seeing such a theatrical performance many years ago. The hypnotist lined up a dozen volunteers, seated in chairs on the stage. He told them that one after another they would find the chair too hot to sit on. They would be compelled to stand, and once standing they would not be able to move. Two or three people in particular would then find that the stage felt hot. Their ability to move would return, but they would have to hop around in their inability to take the heat of the stage. In due course these extraordinary things took place. One after the other the volunteers leapt from their chairs with looks of astonishment, exclaiming that their chairs had become red hot. In recent years this kind of 'act' has been well received on American and British television, but in the bygone days of the variety theatre such bizarre effects were commonly achieved by performers who had mastered the craft of hypnotic suggestion. Consequently, this writer is singularly unimpressed to read of the hysterical laughing and sobbing episodes, and the falling down, trembling and shaking reactions taking place in charismatic conventions where the atmosphere is charged with tension.

Charismatic healer John Wimber writes of his encounter with ten German theological students who questioned elements of his teaching. He invited them to try, by way of experiment, to invite the Holy Spirit to minister healing and renewal to them. He records that they chuckled and said, 'Sure, why not?' To their surprise they experienced extraordinary things which Wimber ascribes to the power of God. He asked one young man, who was rather tall, and standing bolt upright, 'Do you feel anything?' The young man said, 'No, nothing.' John Wimber replied, 'That's strange, because I believe the Holy Spirit is on you. Why don't you sit down?' The young man answered, 'I can't sit down. I can't move. I don't feel anything, and I can't move.'

Was this effect produced by the Holy Spirit? The answer is that we do not read of anything like this in the pages of the New Testament. God has definitely not said that He will work in this way. But the secular theatre has a long tradition of entertaining hypnotists who produce identical effects! However, in the worship and service of the Lord the mind is never bypassed. The Holy Spirit does not work through hypnotic trances and bizarre, unnecessary phenomena when He brings conviction to a needy soul, or when He empowers a believer for service.

In charismatic healing meetings, forces other than the

plain Truth of Scripture are used to produce the desired effects. From start to finish a sequence of hypnotic-suggestion techniques are employed, though often the people conducting these meetings do not realise that they are using suggestion. They are simply copying a procedure which they have seen carried out by others. An atmosphere of expectation is developed; emotional susceptibility is heightened, and the people are told exactly what phenomena will occur.

As the healing session reaches its climax, the Holy Spirit, by some means or other, is 'called down'. Sometimes people are asked to close their eyes and claim their healing. Whatever method is chosen, the moment comes when the illness is commanded to leave in the name of Jesus. Definite effects will be experienced by many people, but usually these turn out to be short-lived. Furthermore, these techniques cannot touch deep-seated, organic disorders, whatever the healers may claim.

It is not by the authority of the Bible that suggestion techniques are used to heal people or to 'prove' the presence of the Holy Spirit. In this kind of thing charismatic workers have returned to the ways of witchcraft and occult religion. The Holy Spirit works by enlightening the *minds* of men and women, and convincing them of the teaching of the Bible. By exercising faith in His promises and His methods alone do we receive a true spiritual blessing. The Holy Spirit *never* bypasses the mind of the believer, and therefore any technique or practice which has been devised by human beings (such as hypnosis), or which is subrational (like modern tongues-speaking), is definitely of the flesh and not of the Spirit.

The mind — which is the rational, thinking faculty — must always be alert and watchful to keep us on the pathway of Truth. However, there is no doubt that charismatic teaching results in a considerable lowering of the credulity threshold of all its adherents. The most shrewd, level-headed kind of person is unavoidably affected by charismatic 'programming'. A tendency to believe incredible things develops, and spiritual discernment falls drastically. The practice of tongues, the relegation of the understanding to a minor place, the diet of miracles, and the extreme subjectivity of charismatic thinking all combine to produce this effect quickly and inevitably.

Once people have been mentally conditioned by a charismatic environment, they are able to take seriously such amazing ideas as Oral Roberts' claim to have seen a vision of Jesus, 900 feet tall. Charismatic practices loosen up the mind in such an unhealthy way that people will believe almost anything.

Once again we refer to Dennis Bennett, writing of the kind of miracles which (he claims) are available to Christians today, if only they will accept charismatic teaching. Mr Bennett quotes David du Plessis, perhaps the best known 'founder' of the modern charismatic movement, who tells of a 'miracle' in his earlier ministry, in which he and some others were gathered at a friend's home, praying for a man who was lying in bed seriously ill about a mile away. 'As we prayed,' says du Plessis, 'the Lord said to me, "You are needed at that bedside right away."' He immediately rushed out of the house and on out of the front gate, and just then the miracle occurred. He records: 'As I took one step out of the gate, my next step fell on the front step of the house a mile away where our sick friend was. It startled me greatly. I know that I was carried that mile instantly because some fifteen minutes later, the rest of the men I had been praying with came puffing down the drive and asked me, "How did you get here so fast?"'

Charismatic books are simply crowded with this kind

of report. Within a few paragraphs of this, Dennis Bennett records how the power and glory of God once lifted an evangelist several feet off the ground in full view of the congregation. The Lord Jesus warned that in the last days false Christs and false prophets would arise, showing great signs and wonders (*Matthew 24.24*). In *2 Thessalonians 2.1-12*, the apostle Paul tells how (just prior to the Lord's return) the 'lawless one' shall be revealed — *whose coming is in accord with the activity of Satan, with all power and signs and false wonders.*

Are we suggesting that the charismatic movement is part of this final delusion? It may well be the preparatory stage, because one of its terrifying effects is that it destroys the spiritual discernment of Christians, making them vulnerable to the devil's powers, signs and lying wonders in the final apostasy. In the meantime the charismatic movement causes God's people to deviate from the true pathway of worship, evangelism and Christian growth.

If Christians believe the unsubstantiated claims of present-day charismatic leaders they will eventually believe anything! If they believe the ludicrous and extravagant yarns of extrovert, ·spiritually-deluded showmen, how will they stand against the lying wonders to be unleashed by the devil during the final apostasy? Will the elect be deceived?

Another charismatic abuse of the mind comes in the form of visions and other direct messages from God, which are now regularly claimed. Charismatic adherents set great store by such messages, which they claim are the words of knowledge or wisdom referred to by Paul. They derive guidance about the will of God from dreams and 'inner impressions', even claiming clairvoyant knowledge of other people's affairs and future events. Sincere believers must be warned away from all this extra-sensory perception because it is scripturally disqualified as a source of spiritual instruction and guidance for today and therefore highly deceptive and dangerous. Instead of the mind being used to receive and understand God's Word, the imagination becomes a trusted source of direct revelation!

We only have to consider how easy it is for the devil to make use of such visions or impressions to add to, distort, or replace the Word of God to realise why they lie at the root of practically all cult errors. In the Old Testament the people of God are warned against false visionaries, and stringent rules are laid down to distinguish between the true and the false.

The Old Testament taught that when the Messiah came to suffer and die for man's sin, all prophecy and visions would be sealed or closed up (see *Daniel 9.24* and the scriptures which are referred to in the chapter — *Is the Word of God Complete?*). The Lord Jesus Christ warned that towards the end of the age loyal believers would be safe in the Truth only while they depended on the revealed Word of God, for there would be a great proliferation of visions and lying wonders.

What kind of people claim to have visions today? Sadly, many sincere believers do, but they must be shown with care and sympathy that they have strayed from the path of God's Word and have fallen into the trap of taking themselves and their natural 'mental impressions' far too seriously.

Some visionaries are just emotionally highly-strung people who have a subconscious need to shock people into listening to them. Others are motivated by spiritual pride and a desire to appear on a higher plane than other believers. These people love to report their 'insights' in mysterious, sanctimonious tones, and to make dramatic pronouncements which cause weak-minded people to admire or envy their prophetic station. Some very evil people use visions as a way of clothing their malicious gossip with the status of 'a word from the Lord'.

However, the very worst visionaries are people who are sold out to Satan, and whose visions are no doubt the result of satanic influence. These are people who bring others under their domination and slavery. This evil class includes such people as the notorious Jonestown murderer, cult founders, extreme charismatic showmen, and vision-claiming popes of Rome. The Lord Jesus has defined His people as those who listen only to His voice, and do not go after the voice of strangers. Any pretensions to visions, now that the Scripture is complete, must be seen as disobedience to Scripture, and we must try to save from this dangerous delusion those earnest believers who have succumbed to charismatic ideas.

10
Is the Holy Spirit In It?

THE MOST BAFFLING characteristic of the modern charismatic movement is its quite amazing capacity for liaison with outright heresy and manifestations of extreme 'worldliness'. Large numbers of charismatics do not seem to care in the least about the compromise which their compatriots court around the world. When it comes to contending for the faith against Romanism, modernism, ecumenism, occult ideas, or this world's Vanity Fair, the charismatic movement is at its weakest and most defective.

The main objective of some of the largest charismatic organisations is openly ecumenical. Pioneers of the movement (Dr David du Plessis and others) have said openly and frequently that they would welcome the emergence of a united world church under the leadership of the Pope. It is their hope that all Protestants and Catholics will be won over to charismatic activities, with the result that they will recognise their essential oneness and the issues which divide them will recede and disappear. It is a tragic fact that world charismatic leaders seem to have no desire to defend the basic evangelical doctrines of the faith, and no readiness at all to keep themselves separate from doctrinal apostasy.

In the light of this, how is it possible for this movement to possess — as it claims — more power and
unction of the Holy Spirit than traditional, non-charismatic Christians? Surely the Holy Spirit is the Holy
Spirit of Truth! Where the Holy Spirit is present there
is bound to be great love and loyalty to the Word of God
coupled with real concern to safeguard and defend it.
Yet the charismatic movement is undeniably indifferent
to the defence of the Bible and its exclusive way of
salvation.

Many charismatic leaders have openly flouted evangelical conversion as the only way to Christ by stating
openly that Roman Catholics and liberals are truly
converted Christians who may receive the gifts of the
Spirit *without changing their beliefs*. This is regardless of
the fact that such people continue to deny justification
by faith alone, and other doctrines essential to true
conversion. Catholic charismatics firmly believe that
salvation is dispensed and administered by the Catholic
Church through the sacraments. Salvation depends on
baptism, the mass, confession, and so on. Leading
charismatic Catholic authors make it very clear that
they aim to strengthen the commitment of faithful
Catholics to their sacraments, to Mary (as an interces-
sor), to the Pope and to the Catholic Church.

There are millions of Roman Catholic charismatics
(Dr David du Plessis says fifty million, and even allowing for exaggeration there must be a vast number).
In fact, Roman Catholic charismatics account for half
the total number of charismatics claimed world-wide.
The Pope has endorsed the Catholic charismatic movement because none of the Catholics involved have
altered their Catholic beliefs. When in 1977 a vast
charismatic congress was held in Kansas City, with
45,000 participants, a Roman Catholic presided and a
great proportion of those present were Catholics. In

1987 a sequel congress took place in New Orleans, attended by most of the major names in the charismatic world, including numerous Catholic priests. Of those who registered, 50% were Catholics. Mass was celebrated every day of the congress, and totally ecumenical sentiments were applauded and endorsed by all throughout the proceedings.

We have already noted that the vast majority of the promoters of extreme Gospel-pop culture are ardent charismatics, as well as devotees of groups on the 'lunatic fringe' of Christendom such as 'Clowns for Christ'. Certainly the most 'worldly' manifestations of evangelicalism in Britain and the USA invariably turn out to be charismatic in viewpoint, as do the very worst of the millionaire 'phonies' making their fortunes on American religious TV shows.

We read of internationally-known charismatic broadcasters using donated funds to build massive luxury homes at fabulous expense. We see their appallingly impious television programmes, programmes sometimes so carnal in character that one cannot believe that there can be any spiritual truth and conscience in those who produce them.

It has been revealed that one internationally-known charismatic healer regularly used special mats on the stage, which enabled him to demonstrate his special power to candidates for healing. Unbeknown to the sick people who mounted the stage to be greeted by this healer, the mats routed electric currents through his body so that each sick person felt a strong tingling sensation on touching the healer's hands.

It is a telling fact that most of the present-day pseudo-Gospel movements of obviously deluded and occult character are strongly charismatic and capable of manifesting all the so-called gifts of the Spirit. The more balanced and earnest charismatics on the sober side of the movement can offer no satisfactory explanation of how gifts which they believe are given by the Holy Spirit can be so easily manifested even by those who turn out to be religious crooks and confidence tricksters.

Viewed world-wide, no Christian movement has shown greater indifference to *Truth* and godly standards than this one. Is the Holy Spirit really in all the tongues, visions, and healings? Is the Holy Spirit vindicating and condoning the shockingly unbiblical antics of so many groups within the charismatic world? Surely not, for it is not the way of the Holy Spirit to work in alliance with error; to blur the difference between 'saved' and 'unsaved'; to promote ecumenism, or to bless worldly lifestyles. He is the Spirit of *holiness* and *Truth*. Sincere evangelicals who have adopted a charismatic position should be greatly exercised by the flagrantly unscriptural stance of the overwhelming majority of charismatic teachers.

Part II
Answering the Questions

MANY BELIEVERS who are not themselves charismatic take the view that charismatic gifts may nevertheless be true blessings sent by God to those who enjoy them. They feel that they should not criticise those of charismatic persuasion, but value them for their distinctive contribution to church life. This neutral attitude seems full of sweet reasonableness and certainly appeals to the irenic disposition of most Christians. However, it is really only an easy way out of a serious problem, for either the charismatic point of view is biblically right, and we are all duty-bound to obey the Lord and subscribe to it, or it is a great mistake, and we should be doing something to persuade our charismatic acquaintances to look at things differently.

Besides this, the matter is one of increasing urgency because the charismatic movement is nowadays very militant. A large section of it is committed to a policy of penetrating orthodox evangelical congregations in order to draw them into the charismatic fold, even if this involves bringing down the existing ministry and leadership, and rending the church asunder.

Many churches which have opted for the hospitable, irenic attitude when faced by charismatic 'invasion'

have found themselves plunged into untold confusion
and deep agony. In addition, charismatics (and extreme
ones at that) have taken over or penetrated many old-
established evangelical institutions — Christian unions,
Bible colleges, periodicals, publishing houses, conventions, missions, and so on. Every way they turn,
evangelicals are confronted by charismatic influence.

The result is that charismatic ideas have already
penetrated the thinking of many non-charismatics far
more than they realise. Large numbers of non-charismatics, for example, now regard as an extreme position
the view that sign-healings and tongues were limited to
the period of New Testament revelation. The fact is
that this view has been the historic position of all the
main Protestant Reformers, churches, confessions and
commentators, apart from Pentecostalists. It is only in
the last twenty or so years that believers outside the
Pentecostal denominations have doubted it. Augustine
described the gifts as 'betokenings' and every major
Bible exegete since has totally agreed.

The following problems are representative of those
which many moderate charismatics and also many
'neutral' Christians raise when the charismatic movement is under discussion. These are the reasons
why they linger in uncertainty, feeling unable to
categorically reject charismatic ideas as mistaken and
unscriptural. Our replies follow the statement of each
problem or query.

11
What About the Signs of Mark 16?

The great commission of the Lord Jesus Christ includes the words recorded in *Mark 16.17-18* — *And these signs will accompany those who have believed: in My name they will cast out demons, they will speak with new tongues; they will pick up serpents, and if they drink any deadly poison, it shall not hurt them; they will lay hands on the sick, and they will recover.* Is this not an unqualified promise to all who believe? If so, then surely such following signs should be expressed in every age?

THE ANSWER TO THIS viewpoint is that the verses quoted, *Mark 16.17-18*, are most certainly *not* part of the great commission applicable to ordinary preachers and believers throughout the ongoing history of the Church. We are put on our guard by the mention of serpents and deadly poisons. No sensible Christian dares to say that the promise of safety when picking up serpents or drinking deadly poison is part of the great commission for all believers. The great commission as recorded in *Matthew 28.18-20* does not include the verses just quoted from *Mark*, and this should guide us in our interpretation of them. The golden rule of interpretation is that we must take account of the *context* of any verse. This certainly helps us to understand the Lord's words about the 'following signs'. The *subject* which dominates these verses is that of the *unbelief* of the disciples.

We pick up the trail in verse 11 where the disciples refuse to believe Mary Magdalene's account of having seen the Lord. Then in verse 13 we find them disbelieving the two disciples to whom the Lord appeared on the Emmaus road. Then in verse 14 we read of how the Lord appears to the eleven, and scolds them for — *their unbelief and hardness of heart, because they had not believed.* The Lord then announces to them the great commission, which applies not only to them, but to all believers who shall follow them.

However, He immediately returns to the problem of their unbelieving tendencies. (This is just what we should expect in view of the 'build up' of this subject in the preceding verses.) Addressing *them* specifically He says that certain signs will follow those of *them* (the eleven) who wholeheartedly believe and obey His instructions. *They* shall cast out devils, speak with new tongues, survive snake bites and poisons, and heal the sick. Signs will follow *these apostles!*

If any of the eleven disciples were to fail to carry out the great commission with wholehearted belief in the Lord's promises, then they would have no part in the wonderful sign-ministries which were to attend the inauguration period of the Church of the Lord Jesus Christ. The final verse of *Mark* records that the disciples obeyed, and reaped the promise.

This exegesis of the passage is totally confirmed by the books of *Acts* and *Hebrews* which inform us that the wonders were principally performed *by the hands of the apostles.* Tongues-speaking certainly went beyond the apostles, but the point of *Mark 16.17-18* is to record that Jesus promised that *all* the sign-ministries would be enjoyed by the apostles if they renounced all mistrust, cynicism and faint-heartedness.

To summarise, the key to the passage lies in *Mark 16.14 — Afterward He appeared to the eleven . . . and He reproached them for their unbelief and hardness of heart.* The principal subject is — the unbelief of the eleven, and the Lord's special promise to them if they repent of this. We must therefore conclude that these words were *specifically* addressed to the eleven, and therefore no present-day believers need lose their assurance because they cannot heal the sick, triumph over venomous snakes or survive deadly poisons!

12
Is Paul's Command Still Binding?

On what basis can it be said that passages of Scripture such as *1 Corinthians 14* are not valid for our day? Surely Paul's words are still binding — *Therefore, my brethren, desire earnestly to prophesy, and do not forbid to speak in tongues*?

How CAN SOME FRIENDS be so certain that this verse is binding in a literal way on Christians today? The scriptural command to honour these gifts clearly applies only so long as the Spirit gives the gifts. If the sovereign Spirit withdraws the gifts, we must not work them up for ourselves by teaching people techniques for speaking in tongues, techniques which, as we have noted previously, work extremely well when they are tried out by non-Christian experimenters!

Some commands in the Bible are obviously intended for temporary situations. This fact greatly alarms some people, but let us take a very elementary and yet irrefutable example. Paul commands the churches to pray for him, that he may open his mouth to speak the Gospel boldly. Obviously we do not dogmatically assert that this command remains literally binding. It was binding only for as long as Paul was alive. After his death, we are not to pray for Paul, but for the *non-inspired* teachers who have taken his place as messengers of Christ. Similarly, now that the temporary gifts of inspired apostles and prophets have passed, we must desire earnestly the fruit of their work, namely the Scriptures, listening with anticipation to every earnest exposition of the Word now fully revealed.

Those who feel bound to take Paul's command literally today, face some remarkable 'omissions' in God's infallible and sufficient Word. Where are the instructions for approving, appointing or recognising prophets and tongues-speakers in the ongoing churches? There are very clear instructions and examples of how to appoint pastors, teachers, elders and deacons, together with detailed descriptions of their qualifications, but there is not a word about any other functionaries.

Outside the *Acts of the Apostles* and *1 Corinthians* there is no mention whatsoever of tongues-speakers. Equally, outside these books the only references to New Testament prophets are in *Ephesians*, and here they are firmly described as part of the initial, foundation stage of the Church *only*.

We must therefore conclude that the scriptural command to honour the sign-gifts applied in its literal form only while the Spirit gave the gifts. For as long as the prophets spoke, their ministry was to be desired and valued. During the period when genuine foreign-language gifts were given, the Spirit was not to be quenched. But the command ceases to be relevant the moment the Holy Spirit withdraws the special gifts.

This does not mean that *1 Corinthians 14* is an irrelevant chapter as far as we are concerned. Not only is it highly important for us to know that the special gifts of early days were exercised within a framework of order, but we are given in this chapter vital instruction on the *principles* of Christian worship for all time. Once the sign-gifts have ceased, the *principles* of edification, peace (ie: a harmonious service), the rule concerning women, and the command that *all things be done properly and in an orderly manner*, will continue to be binding (*1 Corinthians 14.26, 33, 34, 40*). Oddly enough, these are the very principles and rules which are disregarded in so very many charismatic assemblies.

13
Why Should False Gifts Detract from the True?

Should we turn our backs on the charismatic movement because there are extremists? Does the existence of counterfeit coins devalue the genuine article? The doubtfulness of some charismatic claims, and the evident unsoundness of some charismatic teachers, should not discredit this viewpoint. The devil can imitate all gifts, but surely this should not lead us to deny the true gifts?

WHILE IT IS GENERALLY TRUE that everything of value is likely to be counterfeited, this observation should not be too speedily applied to the gifts of the Spirit. After all, these spectacular gifts were intended by God to be very wonderful and impressive *signs*. We must not lose sight of the fact that — *tongues are for a sign*. Similarly, the apostolic healings were extraordinary demonstrations of power which validated the apostles as truly inspired spokesmen of the Lord.

These signs, as originally given, were designed by God to be uniquely efficient and effective as *signs*. The fact is that they were not easily counterfeited, unlike the tame versions of the gifts which we see today. The Lord intended them to be impossible to imitate or counterfeit, as one might expect with signs designed by the infinite and almighty God!

In those days people lived in very small communities — even Corinth being a very small town by today's standards. Ordinary people who had grown up together and who knew one another well suddenly heard some of their number speaking *real* foreign languages which they had never learned. Foreign nationals present would understand them, and other ordinary people would simultaneously be given the miraculous ability to understand and interpret.

The manifestation of tongues in New Testament times was utterly astounding to all. It was wonderful beyond description; a most emphatic and powerful proof of God's presence with the young church. Because the languages were real languages, the early tongues-speakers possessed a sign which has never yet been reproduced by any cult or group in the world either before or since. As far as the testimony of history is concerned, *true* tongues-speaking does not appear to be counterfeitable at all.

Today's tongues however, not being real foreign languages, are very easily 'achieved' by everyone, from non-Christian religious groups to cynical students engaging in experiments! The people speaking in tongues never know what their words mean, and if there is an interpreter, he is the only person present who thinks he knows the meaning, and so there is never any corroborative aspect to the exercise. Where is the *sign* value of this?

Nowadays the tongues-speaker is obliged to appeal to our faith to rescue his 'sign' from being confused with the glossolalia of non-Christian cults! There is no apparent difference. So can this really be the kind of sign that God would have created in order to rebuke and humble the unbelieving Jews of Bible times? Would the

Lord use a sign which contained no evidence of divine power, evoked distaste and cynicism, and depended on goodwill and faith for its acceptance?

The godly Pentecostalist asks us to recognise his gifts as being different from those manifested by the extremists and con-men of the charismatic movement, as well as those of non-Christian cults. We naturally extend brotherly recognition to every Pentecostalist who is a sincere disciple of the Lord, but we cannot easily extend the same recognition and respect to his gifts, because they are indistinguishable from those of the cults. We ask again, is it possible that God would have given signs so lacking in the obvious stamp of divine power that they would end up buried and lost amidst a welter of counterfeit 'gifts'? A sign is surely like a precious key. If it can be easily fabricated by a criminal it is a poor design. Even worse, if it can be easily made by a casual visitor, then it is an utterly worthless design.

The original gifts were awe-inspiring, riveting, and not at all easy to imitate. The present-day gifts are perplexing phenomena which prove nothing and can be duplicated with relative ease by Christians and non-Christians alike. The vast scale on which 'unknown-language', ecstatic tongues-speaking has occurred among non-Christian groups down the centuries must very obviously discredit this activity as the rightful successor of biblical tongues-speaking.

When the Lord Jesus Christ, as part of His sign-ministry, cast out devils, He was able to throw down the challenge to His critics, *By whom do your sons cast them out?* The point was that the Jews could not cast them out no matter what methods they tried. Only the Lord could cast out demons at a word, and thus He employed a sign which no one could copy or counterfeit. It is surely wrong to make the comfortable assumption that the presence of counterfeit tongues need not worry us or dampen our belief that some of the gifts may be genuine. This is a totally unsound and inappropriate assumption when we are dealing with signs *designed by the Lord*. The true sign-gifts of Bible times were quite outstanding, and not susceptible to forgery.

14
Why Not Return
to Early Church Life?

Surely the picture given in the New Testament is of churches which constantly enjoyed miracles and tongues-speaking. Why should these blessings be relegated to the past?

IS IT TRUE THAT tongues-speaking and healing were so very common in New Testament times? This is a vital question because it is completely taken for granted by charismatic teachers that virtually everyone spoke in tongues and that healings were everyday occurrences in the early church. The reality of the situation is that only three occurrences of tongues-speaking are recorded in *Acts*, in chapters 2, 10-11 and 19, and apart from the instructions given in *1 Corinthians* there is no further mention of tongues-speaking anywhere in the New Testament.

It is generally accepted by all evangelicals that some believers continued to be given inspiration to speak in tongues between these recorded events, so that other Jews could also have witnessed God's sign. However, even this is no more than an assumption, and it is an even greater assumption to suppose that *numerous* Christians spoke in tongues *constantly*. The three references in *Acts* do not support this notion at all. In each of the recorded cases of tongues-speaking some special authentication was called for to support the message preached. In each case Jews were involved — Jews who needed to see that the old Jewish order had been terminated, and that Jews and Gentiles were now together in a new church, ruled directly by the Holy Spirit. The tongues-speaking incident of *Acts 10* is an example. Peter had just been shown by God, through a vision, that he could associate with Gentiles. Taking a band of converted Jews with him he visited the house of Cornelius. God was about to take him a step further, and show him that Gentiles were his *equals* in the Gospel.

As Peter preached to Cornelius (and his God-fearing Gentile friends) the Holy Spirit fell upon them, as Luke relates: *And all the circumcised believers who had come with Peter were amazed, because the gift of the Holy Spirit had been poured out upon the Gentiles also. For they were hearing them speaking with tongues and exalting God. Then Peter answered, 'Surely no one can refuse the water for these to be baptized who have received the Holy Spirit just as we did, can he?'* (Acts 10.45-47).

The purpose of this tongues manifestation was to unlock the minds of converted Jews to the fact that Gentiles could be true converts and fellow members in Christ. When Peter later reported back to the Jewish Christians in the church at Jerusalem, he said something very remarkable which strongly suggests that there had not been very much (if any) tongues-speaking between Pentecost and the outpouring of the Spirit in the house of Cornelius which occurred more than eight years later! Peter said — *And as I began to speak, the Holy Spirit fell upon them, just as He did upon us at the beginning. And I remembered the word of the Lord, how He used to say, 'John baptized with water, but you shall be baptized with the Holy Spirit'* (Acts 11.15-16). This was clearly only the second time Peter had witnessed a 'group outpouring' of the Spirit since Pentecost. Peter, and the Jews with him at the house of Cornelius, had been amazed that the same phenomenon occurred which they remembered from years before.

The only other record of tongues-speaking in *Acts* occurs in *Acts 19.6.* Here Paul found twelve Jewish people who were devout believers in the message of John the Baptist. They had a sincere (but pre-Christian) hope in the Messiah. When they gladly embraced the full understanding of the Gospel, Paul laid his hands on them and they spoke in tongues and prophesied. Clearly God gave them these signs as a kind of 'mini-Pentecost'. First, being disciples of John they had needed to be brought up to date on Calvary and the resurrection. Then, as Jews they needed to learn (like Peter and the Jews of Jerusalem) that a totally new day had dawned, a new order had come in, and a new church had been inaugurated under the rule of the Holy Spirit. Once again, therefore, there was a special purpose in the gift of tongues — fully in accordance with Paul's teaching that tongues are primarily a sign for the Jews.

Let us then be very careful before allowing ourselves to be swept away by the romantic idea that tongues-speaking was an everyday and normal feature of the life and worship of the New Testament churches. Anyone and everyone — it is claimed — used tongues both publicly and privately. This concept is simply not in line with the facts of the *Acts* record, as any reader can judge. There may well have been many more occurrences of tongues-speaking than those recorded, but the fact remains that only three incidents are spoken of in *Acts*, and we should not therefore read the modern charismatic scene into the Scriptures.

The church at Corinth was blessed with a number of tongues-speakers, but as an absolute maximum of three tongues messages were permitted in their service, the number of gifted people was probably quite small. Women were not permitted to speak at all. The popular charismatic idea of constant tongues simply cannot be reconciled with the data provided in the Bible.

The same goes for the frequency of healing miracles, for once again a huge discrepancy has arisen between assumption and reality. Healing acts were certainly numerous and spectacular, but according to *Acts* they were *exclusively* carried out by the apostles and those who worked with them (and who received their power or gift from the apostles). Paul tells us that the healing miracles which he performed were *signs of an apostle*. Because he did these things, the believers at Corinth and elsewhere could be sure that he was a true apostle. He reminds them of this in *2 Corinthians 12.11-12 — In no respect was I inferior to the most eminent apostles . . . The signs of a true apostle were performed among you . . . by signs and wonders and miracles.*

If ordinary pastors and church members had been able to perform healings, then Paul would never have been able to authenticate his apostleship as he did. We can be certain, therefore, that the mighty sign-healings of those days, however numerous, were confined to the apostles and those who they expressly nominated.

Tongues and healings were not therefore widely practised by ordinary believers as most charismatic teachers assume. Judging from most of the epistles, it would seem that churches in many cities never experienced tongues-speaking at all. Evidently this sign to the Jews was not necessary in every place. When charismatic writers explain Scripture passages they always assume a picture of the early church as being constantly engaged in signs, wonders and tongues, but this presupposition bears no relation to the real facts of the biblical record. The charismatic view of the early church is nothing more than fantasy!

15
Does God Heal Today?

Are not the healing miracles of Christ and His apostles intended as a pattern for the kind of things which present-day churches ought to be doing? Is there no ministry of divine healing for today?

GOD OFTEN HEALS people from their sicknesses, but we must understand that there are two different kinds of healing in God's dealings with mankind. There were once those spectacular, undeniable, sign-miracle healings, which had a specific purpose. Their purpose was to confirm the authenticity of a messenger from God. But there is also another kind of healing which has nothing to do with signs, or the authentication of anyone. *James 5.14-16* describes this other kind of healing — *Is anyone among you sick?* [The Greek word implies very, very sick.] *Let him call for the elders of the church, and let them pray over him, anointing him with oil in the name of the Lord; and the prayer offered in faith will restore the one who is sick, and the Lord will raise him up . . . Pray for one another, so that you may be healed.*

We are not told by James to call for a 'gifted' healer, but to call for the appointed elders of our church, godly men from the same local body of believers who know and love us, and they will pray. Then God in His sovereignty, according to His will, not according to our will, will determine how, when, where or whether the sick Christian will become better. Notice carefully, that the passage does not say how the sick person shall be raised up. It does not say how long it will take. It does not say whether or not medicines will be needed, or nurses, doctors, hospitals, or convalescence.

The question may be asked — If the person is raised up, how do we know God did it? We know because this healing is a family affair within and among God's people. It is not for show; it is not a sign to the world. It does not need to be 'undeniable'. It is something within the body of Christ for the encouragement of God's people.

There is nothing in *James* 5 which has anything to do with sign-miracles or gifted healers. The passage does, however, teach us that God is aware of, and concerned about, and involved in, sickness among His people, and it gives His prescribed way to cope with this problem.

As we look at *James* 5, with its gracious possibilities for healing in answer to prayer, let us remember that the outcome is in accordance with the sovereign will of God. We must bear in mind that the New Testament is filled with examples of great and godly men who prayed earnestly for physical healing but did not receive it. Take the apostle Paul. Surely, without controversy, he was one of the greatest Christians who has ever lived since the Day of Pentecost, yet Paul was constantly afflicted with physical limitations. He suffered that thorn in the flesh — how we would like to know what it was. But God does not want us to know so that we can more easily substitute our own physical handicap for Paul's example.

What did Paul do about his thorn? He did the right thing. He did not demand a healing from God, nor did he use God's special sign-gift which he possessed as an apostle to heal himself. He just prayed earnestly, in faith, to the Lord Jesus Christ, the sovereign Head of the Church, 'Lord, remove this thorn from my flesh; it is painful; it is inconvenient; it is hindering to my ministry. Please remove the thorn.'

However, nothing happened, though he prayed on three distinct occasions. What was God's answer? *My grace is sufficient for you.* Paul's response was — *Most gladly, therefore, I will rather boast about my weaknesses, that the power of Christ may dwell in me . . . for when I am weak, then I am strong.*

Here is the paradox of all Christian life and ministry: when we are helpless, when we are at our worst, when we have nothing in ourselves to depend upon, then the Lord Jesus Christ can manifest in a unique way that it is He Who does the work. *Apart from Me* — He said — *you can do nothing.* Our health, strength and vigour do not provide the effective means by which God will build His church.

What a devastating blow Paul's infirmity is to the theology of the modern faith-healing movement which claims that our physical ailments are an exact measurement of our *lack of faith* in Jesus Christ's atoning work, which, they say, provided for our healing. The greatest saints in the history of the Church include many who have been helpless, hopeless cripples, and blind saints who have never been healed. The case of Joni — a young lady in the United States who was paralysed from the neck down — is now well known. For a brief season, as you read in her remarkable book, she was led to believe that by faith she could be instantly healed. This was one of the most tragic periods of her life, and she discovered from a careful, prayerful study of Scripture that the idea was a total deception.

In the light of *Acts 19*, we may say that the apostle Paul was an expert at healing people supernaturally.

On the basis of this, many charismatic faith-healers in America will appeal on their radio programmes for portions of garments to be sent to them, preferably with some money attached! The garment will be prayed over and sent back to the sender (without the money) and healing will be guaranteed, subject to this qualification — your healing will be accomplished in proportion to your faith. In other words, it is not the healer's responsibility whether or not anything happens, and no one will get their money back if there is no healing. What a travesty of the New Testament! What blasphemy! What a perversion of the unique sign-miracle ministries of the apostles!

The charismatic movement has failed to distinguish between the two kinds of healing clearly revealed in the Bible, namely, authenticating sign-miracle healing performed by the hands of temporary apostles, and the ongoing kind of healing described in *James 5*. This is our healing ministry for today, but it is of a quite different style and order from the ministry of sign-miracles.

16
Surely We Must Exorcise Demons?

Demonic powers assaulted the church in the first century and presumably continue to do so in our twentieth century. In the light of this, is not the charismatic ministry of exorcism valid and necessary?

THE CASTING OUT of demons is certainly a central feature of charismatic activity, but one which actually runs counter to many passages of Scripture. To begin with, the Bible teaches that since the coming of Christ people can no longer be occupied by demons *against their will*, but only as the result of their voluntary interference and co-operation with the spirit world. Thus demon possession has become greatly reduced in frequency, and virtually confined to circles of occult commitment.

Charismatics, however, see demon possession everywhere, casting demons out of people who manifest none of the 'symptoms' present in biblical descriptions of possession, apart from the 'programmed' hysterical reaction which is sometimes seen in charismatic adherents who are being exorcised.

In brief, the biblical case against 'involuntary' demon possession is as follows:

(1) Jesus taught that His coming would lead to a severe curtailment of Satan's powers to possess souls (*Luke 11.20-22; John 12.31*).

(2) Demons themselves were aware of the impending end of their freedom to possess souls (*Luke 8.28; Mark 1.24*).

(3) Demons are described as being in captivity since Calvary, for Christ has stripped them of their unrestricted power to possess the minds and souls of people (*Ephesians 4.8; Psalm 68.18*).

(4) No open manifestation of Satan (and demons) is to be allowed until the end of the age. He must work chiefly by secrecy and stealth; by temptation and lies. He is forced to remain invisible in his operation — something which would not be the case if demons were still allowed to become virtually 'incarnate' at their whim in large numbers of people (*2 Thessalonians 2.6-8*).

(5) The ongoing activities of demons are quite concisely described in various New Testament passages, and the occupying of souls is not a listed activity. They lie, tempt, stir up discord in the church, make war with the church, persecute and constantly seek to plant false doctrines (eg: *1 Timothy 4.1; James 3.14-15; 1 John 4.1-6; Revelation 12.17*).

(6) We certainly have the *record* of sign-miracle exorcisms being carried out by the Lord and His apostles, but there is not one word of *command* or instruction addressed to ordinary ministers and believers giving them the authority to exorcise demons. Equally, nothing is said in the Pastoral Epistles, or the long passages in *Romans*, *Galatians* and *Ephesians* which deal with satanic activity and temptation.

We conclude that demon possession will be a comparatively rare form of human tragedy. If we are confronted with a rare case of possession what should we do? We should follow the principle that Christ the Lord is alone able to free the exploited, possessed soul, and we must urge that person to go to Christ for release. We can no more liberate a demon-possessed soul than we can regenerate a soul! We can *do* nothing, except plead with men and women to go to Christ — the only High Priest — for *all* their afflictions of soul.

No believer should arrogate to himself Christ's priestly powers and seek to effect any kind of deliverance. No believer should ever attempt to personally interact with a demon, for to do so is a grave violation of the command of God which forbids commerce and dialogue with the forces of darkness (*Leviticus 20.27; Deuteronomy 18.10-12*).

The teaching of the New Testament is that our fight against Satan and his hosts is an *indirect* conflict. We do not touch, feel, speak with, or *directly* engage the enemy, but we fight by using the armour and weaponry which God provides (see *Ephesians 6.10-18*). As he tempts us we engage in the spiritual duties which protect us, and we fight back, not by verbally lashing out at demons, but by spreading the Gospel and thus winning over the hearts of men and women.

Many charismatic healers think that exorcism is a necessary part of healing, because Satan (or an oppressing demon) is behind all illness. But nowhere in the New Testament are Satan or demons said to be responsible for illness — except in the case of those people who were fully demon possessed. In all these matters the 'new theology' of charismatic teachers is extremely superficial and young believers need to be warned of this.

We must remember that the chief activity of demons against the people of God now is to infiltrate churches with doctrines invented by demons! What a terrible irony it is that while Satan works on unhindered in spreading false teaching, many of the Lord's people are fighting the battle of 2,000 years ago by 'casting out' imaginary demons!*

*The arguments described here are explained more fully in *The Healing Epidemic*, Peter Masters (Wakeman Trust, London).

17
If Preaching Is Inspired, Why Not Prophecy?

Non-charismatic preachers look for an anointing of the Spirit on their preaching, so why deny the gifts of prophecy and words of knowledge to charismatic people? Traditional preaching, helped by the Spirit, always contains prophetic elements (God's message for the present time). What is the difference between this and words of knowledge?

THIS KIND OF THINKING represents a very precarious and hazardous grasp of the supreme and exclusive authority of Scripture, and those who feel this way are advised to give much more thought to the great principle of the Reformation — *sola scriptura* — Scripture alone! They may not be aware of it, but they have already absorbed a highly charismatic (even Quaker-like) concept of revelation which is completely contrary to the Bible's teaching about itself as the exclusive source of spiritual knowledge for the Church of Christ on earth.

Certainly the illumination and help of the Spirit are essential if we are to grasp the teaching of God's Word. But absolutely everything which is necessary for salvation, faith and life is already set down in the Scripture, and nothing can be added to it either by new revelation or by human wisdom. The terms 'prophecy' and 'words of knowledge' suggest that spiritual knowledge of all manner of things may be directly infused into the minds of 'gifted' teachers or preachers. They also suggest that such teachers receive insights and interpretations of Scripture which 'ungifted' teachers will never see.

Those who hold such views believe that the Bible is only *part* of God's communicating process. They think that God uses the Bible *plus* teachers directly gifted with knowledge and insight. But God has given His Word to be the *one and only objective test* of all our ideas, opinions, teachings, thoughts and actions. Furthermore, He has made it so efficient and plain as a means of expressing His will that all true Christians (possessing converted, enlightened minds) may confidently appeal to its plain meaning as the final arbiter in all disputes.

God has not arranged matters so that we depend upon certain privileged individuals who possess the 'gift of knowledge', and who alone can tell us the Bible's meaning. This has always been the claim of Rome, but not of Protestantism. Amongst charismatic believers it is a new, subtle and very dangerous form of priestcraft and elitism. As the 1689 *Baptist Confession* states — 'The infallible rule of interpretation of Scripture is the Scripture itself, and therefore when there is a question about the true and full sense of any Scripture . . . it must be searched by other passages which speak more clearly. The supreme judge, by which all controversies of religion are to be determined . . . can be no other than the holy Scripture . . . and in the sentence of Scripture we are to rest.'

The biblical pastor-teacher is someone who explains and expounds the Word of God, not someone who has a direct channel of revelation from God, or exclusive light from God in any form whatsoever. The prophet is in the past; the teacher of God's settled, completed and established Word is God's instrument today.

This is affirmed by the words of the apostle Peter (written about AD 66, towards the end of the New Testament revelation) — *But false prophets also arose among the people, just as there will also be false teachers among you . . . (2 Peter 2.1).* Here *prophets* are already being replaced by *teachers*, a fact reflected in the Pastoral Epistles which instruct the ongoing church about the appointment of teachers, but not about the appointment or recognition of prophets.

When a Christian teacher explains anything, he is in no *personal* sense a prophet, but merely a representative of the supreme Prophet, the Lord Jesus Christ. Thus no teaching is in the least 'prophetic' unless it is scriptural teaching. Sometimes, in describing a preacher, people use the word 'prophetic' as a synonym for 'inspiring' or 'apposite'. This use of the word is unwise enough, but it is even worse when people really mean to impute an element of direct inspiration to the messages of preachers. The 'anointing' of a preacher makes him bold, feelingful, sympathetic, jealous for the glory of God, diligent and efficient in his searching of the Scripture, and perhaps also passionate and fluent in the delivery of his message. It does not convey to him special revelation. Therefore the 'anointing' which is sought by the traditional evangelical preacher cannot be used as justification for charismatic gifts of prophecy.

18
Do Not the Gifts
Stay Until Christ Comes?

**If *1 Corinthians 13.10 (but when the perfect comes, the
partial will be done away)* refers not to the completing
of the Bible, but to the second coming of Christ, then
the gifts will not pass away until the Lord comes. As
practically all the great commentators of the past take
the view that Paul refers to the coming of Christ, should
we not expect the gifts to be present until the end?**

IT IS TRUE THAT a number of *non*-charismatic teachers
of recent times have adopted an interpretation of Paul's
words which says that the phrase *when the perfect comes*
refers to the completion of New Testament revelation.
According to this view, as soon as the Bible was perfect
and complete, then the gifts of prophecy, tongues-
speaking and 'inspired' knowledge vanished away. This
interpretation is, however, extremely controversial and
many non-charismatics (as well as pro-charismatics)
find it hard to swallow.

It is equally true that the great commentaries of the
past mostly take the view that Paul is referring to the
end of the age when the Lord shall come to bring in the
eternal age of perfection.

If we prefer to take this older interpretation, does it

then follow that charismatic gifts will last all the way to the end of the age? Certainly not, because Paul is speaking about the revealed *knowledge* which revelatory gifts produced, not about the gifts themselves. The end-product of the gifts was revealed Truth. But, says Paul, even the revealed Truth of the Bible is not totally complete, and when the Lord comes it will be eclipsed and superseded by the full light of Heaven!

If we examine Paul's words carefully we find that it is only that which *we know* and that which *we prophesy* which is timed to pass away when the Lord comes. Tongues will certainly cease, but Paul does not say when. He does not mention tongues when he puts a date on the ending of all revealed knowledge. So, the apostle's words leave room for the gift of tongues to cease at a much earlier date than the Lord's return, namely, the end of the inaugural period of the Church.

Many commentators allow for the fact that Paul *may* (in *1 Corinthians 13.8*) be including *tongues* with *knowledge* as things which will last until the end of the age. But these commentators say that Paul is no longer speaking about languages which are given as a gift, but about the *natural* speaking of languages throughout the world. So, he simply says — 'All languages shall end.' Let us follow the reasoning of the apostle, according to this interpretation:—

Paul is trying to help the Corinthians to get the gift of tongues into perspective. To reinforce his case he points out that *all* human languages will be done away with anyway in the eternal glory. In other words he says, 'Why do you make so much of those to whom God gives the gift of speaking in another language? The time will come when *all* earth's different languages will be abolished, and then all redeemed people will speak the one language of Heaven.' Calvin takes this view of the passage, saying: 'Since learning, knowledge of languages, and similar gifts serve the needs of this life, it does not seem to me that they will remain in existence when that time comes.'

Neither of these two views of the passage lend any weight to the idea that the gift of tongues will remain in force to the end of the age. Yet these views represent virtually the only seriously-held understandings of Paul's words until very recent times. The fact is that in verses 8-9 Paul does not specifically link the ending of tongues with the end of the age, so the passage provides no support whatsoever for the charismatic interpretation of his words, namely, that tongues and other charismatic gifts continue until Christ comes.

19
What About Tongues in Personal Devotions?

Does not Paul say in *1 Corinthians 14* — *One who speaks in a tongue does not speak to men, but to God*? And does he not add — *One who speaks in a tongue edifies himself*? If, therefore, tongues are a legitimate form of prayer, and also a means of being edified, what right do we have to disparage such a gift?

THIS VIEW OF *1 Corinthians 14.2 & 4* misses the whole point of what Paul is saying in these verses. He goes to great lengths to show that tongues-speaking is completely without purpose unless the utterance is interpreted so that all the people can understand. We have already examined this issue in the chapter, *Tongues Were Never for Personal Benefit*, but it is well worth clarifying the issue further. Paul has already made clear (in *1 Corinthians 12.7*) that each gift is intended to minister to *everyone* in the church. Contrary to this principle, some tongues-speakers were omitting to secure an interpreter to validate their messages and relate them to the assembled church. Paul is in fact rebuking such people when he says that they only edify themselves. Only *they* benefit from God's message.

As we have noted previously, Paul's words also carry

a most important implication which completely invalidates the present-day charismatic use of tongues. He shows that the tongues-speaker normally understood his own foreign-language message. Note carefully his words — *One who speaks in a tongue edifies himself*. We repeat that the Greek word for *edify* (lit: to build up) refers to the conscious gaining of knowledge. Paul's complaint is that some Corinthian tongues-speakers were receiving genuine messages from the Lord which they understood, and which added to their personal knowledge, but unfortunately they were not translating these messages and so they were keeping them to themselves. Paul is opposed to this and rebukes them. After all, these messages were not meant for the speakers alone, but for all the church. (See *1 Corinthians 12.7* and *14.5*.)

Today, many people think that the tongues-speaker is not meant to understand his tongue, but that understanding is the sole prerogative of the interpreter! The tongues-speaker is evidently 'edified' in some mysterious, intangible manner — emotionally perhaps — though the Greek word *edify (oikodomeo)*, as used in the Bible, does not permit this idea.

The present-day tongues-speaker is never edified in the proper sense of the term because he derives no intelligible message from the words he utters. His understanding is unfruitful because his mind receives no tangible instruction unless an interpreter speaks. Therefore, he can never be in the position described by Paul, in which a tongues-speaker, even though there is no interpreter — *edifies himself*.

When a tongues-speaker does not intelligently understand his own gift-language and message, the so-called 'gift' must certainly be called into question. We have a duty to protect one another from falling under the power of any experience or influence (including the influence of our own imaginations and emotions) other than that of wholesome and comprehensible impressions made on the conscious mind.

'Praying in a tongue' is based on a mistaken view of *1 Corinthians 14.2* where Paul says, *One who speaks in a tongue does not speak to men, but to God.* Here Paul points out that a tongues-speaker who fails to interpret his message puts himself in the extraordinary position of preaching to God. Only the Lord can understand what he is saying. This ought to raise eyebrows, because the sole purpose of tongues (as Paul keeps saying) is to bring a message *from* God *to* the whole assembly. Tongues-speaking is a message from God to people. If God gives a message only to find that He is the only listener, then something has obviously gone radically wrong! This is what Paul is explaining. He is not giving sanction to the practice of praying to God in a tongue.

Another misunderstood text is *1 Corinthians 14.14* where Paul says — *For if I pray in a tongue, my spirit prays, but my mind is unfruitful.* Paul does not mean to say that it is possible to pray in a tongue. On the contrary, he is saying that if anyone receives a message in a tongue which he does not understand, then he must pray for understanding, because *everything* must be done with the understanding. Whatever we do in the worship of God, says Paul, whether praying or singing, must be done with the understanding. Consider the apostle's words: *Therefore let one who speaks in a tongue pray that he may interpret. For if I pray in a tongue, my spirit prays, but my mind is unfruitful. What is the outcome then? I shall pray with the spirit and I shall pray with the mind also; I shall sing with the spirit and I shall sing with the mind also (1 Corinthians 14.13-15).*

Paul, then, does not advocate the use of tongues in prayer. Rather he shows how absurd it is to speak in a tongue which we do not understand, by showing how foolish it would be if we were to pray this way. What would we be asking for? What would we be giving thanks for? What would we be saying in praise to God? The answer is — we don't know! Thus prayer would become a nonsense. And by this illustration, the apostle invalidates any tongues-message which the speaker is not enabled to understand.

20
Snares of Satan

THE QUESTION IS often asked — If today's prophecies, visions and tongues are not from God, are they inspired by the devil? Some people seem to think that it must be one or the other. This is simply not the case. Godly believers make many mistakes, but it does not follow that the devil is directly inspiring them. A believer may take a wrong route on a journey, but no one suggests that the mistake is made by the direct intervention of Satan. Sometimes a believer may become emotionally overwrought, hear noises in the night, and — under very great stress — even suffer hallucinations, but all these experiences may be explained without supposing that the person has a demon.

Large numbers of people who speak in unintelligible tongues do so *because* they are sincere believers who have been taught that God wants them to do this. In their sincerity they have striven to obey, agonising and longing for the 'gift'. Most have also received coaching to help them speak in tongues. Charged with a powerful desire and need to give utterance it is almost inevitable that they will, sooner or later, do so.

As far as sincere believers are concerned, tongues-speaking is no more from the devil than any other semi-voluntary, hyper-excited reaction of the human mind or body, though the ecstatic trances of extreme charismatic experiences may certainly expose people to demonic interference.

Present-day healings are to be explained in terms of both imagined healings, and short-lived relief from sickness due to the powerful influence of the mind over the body. Demonic power is not necessarily involved, although it may be that some charismatic false teachers derive help from the powers of darkness, just as cult teachers do.

Nevertheless, while we affirm that the more sincere charismatic believers are not necessarily under any form of satanic influence in their erroneous practices, they undoubtedly make themselves highly vulnerable to temptation. Under the influence of charismatic teaching people learn to trust in ecstatic experiences, impulses, coincidences, and a host of other subjective influences. The devil soon takes advantage of such people. They quickly come to trust their impulses as the direct guidance of God, and many progress to receiving all their guidance through dreams and visions.

In the closing pages of his book, *Tongues: To Speak or Not to Speak*, Dr Donald Burdick refers to the benefits which many sincere charismatics believe they have gained from tongues-speaking. They say that they have found a renewed love for the Lord, an intensely personal relationship with Him, and a stronger desire for prayer. They have regained emotion in their spiritual lives, and the Holy Spirit has become for them a prominent member of the Godhead. Their inner conflicts and tensions have been reduced.

However, all these benefits are available to believers, according to Scripture, without the need to speak in tongues. If tongues-speakers have gained these benefits it is due to their underlying spiritual desire for them —

not to their tongues-speaking. Modern tongues-speaking will only confuse the issue and lead the believer down a false and dangerous path, because it is a psychological substitute for a supernatural experience. As Dr Burdick says, it is something bordering on the psychopathic for it is a product of the brain when it is detached from rational control. It is 'toying with this delicate, precious instrument which God has given us'.

Tongues-speaking and all other forms of charismatic emotional abandonment are bound to lead to a substitution of sight for faith as believers seek tangible evidence of God's presence, rather than being willing to take it by faith. They will lead them away from obtaining their inspiration and consolation from the Word and promises of God, leaving them at the mercy of subjective impressions. In short, it is the most unkind and dangerous method believers could possibly employ to seek their desired spiritual blessings.

By now there are very many believers who have passed into and out of a charismatic experience. For a time they were deeply affected by the closed-eyes and raised-hands mode of worship and the uninhibited expressions of emotion in response to (or so it seemed) the moving of the Spirit. The exuberance of the worship and the closeness of relationships won them over. The experience of worshipping in tongues — yielding to the ecstatic flow of heavenly language — appealed to them as a marvellous form of 'release'.

Eventually, however, they came to realise that the general outlook of their charismatic group was far from the plain teaching of the Word of God. As they studied the Word they began to be disturbed by the constant flow of prophecies, and they increasingly found the doctrinal grasp of charismatic teachers to be superficial and spiritually unsatisfying. Many have been shocked by the growing extremism of recent years, especially by the wild and extravagant claims connected with exorcism and healing.

Ex-charismatics have spoken of their disillusionment over the lack of real concern for righteousness and holiness. They have found that the baptism-of-the-Spirit formula for sanctification did not really touch their lives and bring them power over their sins. Many have singled out for criticism the charismatic style of worship, with its emphasis on emotional abandonment. With the passing of time they found it all very repetitive, even banal, and it became painfully apparent to them that this kind of worship seldom rose beyond an elementary and highly subjective view of salvation. The overall lack of awe and reverence coupled with the unashamed use of worldly-idiom rhythmic music became jarring and offensive to them, and their souls ached and longed for something deeper, more substantial, more reverent, more objective, more divine.

Another cause of dissatisfaction expressed by ex-charismatics is the incessant tendency for exaggeration, seen in the constant claims of amazing wonders, totally divorced from reality. Most of all, ex-charismatics, profess their relief at being out of an atmosphere in which they developed an almost total dependence upon feelings, experiences, thrills, miracles, impulses and coincidences.

In these days of spiritual confusion, God is calling upon His people to stand fast in the true doctrine of the Spirit — the teaching which has undergirded the worship and witness of Christ's people throughout this Gospel age. At the time of the Reformation, real spiritual power purged many Western nations of superstition and of doctrines of demons, so that people no longer lived in fear of their shadows in subjection to the fables of Rome. But now the tide has turned and Satan's day of vengeance is at hand. Through the charismatic movement, the people of Christ have themselves become the advocates of practices only a hair's breadth from witchcraft and sorcery. Never before have Bible-believing people so needed the exhortations of old:—

Stand firm and hold to the traditions which you were taught (2 Thessalonians 2.15);

Hold fast until I come (Revelation 2.25).

My Search for Charismatic Reality
Neil Babcox

The author writes in the preface to this book: 'I have written this book for those who have the courage to examine their faith, though the process of doing so may prove to be disturbing... My testimony is this. I have come to believe that certain experiences of mine related to such spiritual gifts as speaking in tongues and prophecy were not authentic. This book is the record of the struggles that led me to adopt this conclusion.'

Throughout this book the sincerity of the author's soul-searching is evident. The sympathetic tone and the emphasis on personal testimony makes this an ideal book for charismatic readers, and also for non-charismatic readers who wish to gain insight into the thoughts and emotions surrounding tongues utterances and prophecies. 91 pages, paperback.

The Healing Epidemic
Peter Masters

'Spiritual healing — carried out by gifted people — is being promoted in Christian circles as never before. We can no longer be interested in divine healing simply out of personal curiosity. The fact is that healing has become the chief attraction and propaganda tool of a new, crusading Pentecostalism which wants to permeate and engulf traditional Bible Christianity.'

The author deals directly with the methods of John Wimber, Yonggi Cho and others such as Colin Urquhart and Jim Glennon showing how their methods and claims undermine the Word of God and even challenge the Deity of Christ. He exposes the occult foundation of a great deal of present-day charismatic healing practice and refutes the many claims of casting out demons.

On the positive side a chapter outlines the many texts for answering pro-healing arguments. Another chapter surveys the Bible passages on revelatory and sign gifts, reaffirming the cessation of the miraculous gifts in the apostolic era. A further chapter presents in helpful detail the correct way to pray for healing as set out in *James 5*. 227 pages, paperback.

Prof Verna Wright MD FRCP, a medical professor at Leeds University Medical School and a leading Rheumatologist provides a medical assessment of modern miracle healers. 227 pages, paperback.